# WISDOM FOR FAMILY LIVING

DAWN J. BARRIE

Grandma has written "Wisdom for Family Living' with passion and a heart from her own knowledge of life, to help others understand the importance of having a biblical-centred family life in today's world.

Over a lifetime, she has seen how family life has moved away from God as the views of the world have changed. She explains that even though this has happened, today, there is more reason than ever to have faith and trust in God to guide us in our marriages, raising our children and our finances.

*Kendall and Ruth H., Andrew and Sarah M., Josh and Tegan B.*

My Grandmother has lived a life with strong values in God, and with kindness, patience, and resilience, and this book reflects her values. The time and care she has taken to write these words is a tribute to the love she has for her Lord and family. I pray it encourages others as much as she has encouraged me.

*Breanna.*

In 'Wisdom for Family Living', Dawn beautifully illustrates how life's challenges can become opportunities to strengthen family unity and grow in faith. With practical, faith-based insights, this book offers an honest guide for those seeking to build a marriage and family life grounded in God-honouring biblical truths.

*Josh and Anna Forrest.*

Rich in experience and rooted in Scripture, this book is like sitting down with a wise grandmother, sharing truths we need but often miss in today's world. My friend's life and words overflow with genuine faith and practical insight, offering readers a timeless gift of wisdom for every season.

*Rev. Seb Henley.*

Ark House Press
arkhousepress.com

© 2024 DAWN J. BARRIE

All rights reserved. Apart from any fair dealing for the purpose of study, research, criticism, or review, as permitted under the Copyright Act, no part may be reproduced by any process without written permission.

Unless otherwise stated, all Scriptures are taken from the New International Translation (Holy Bible. Copyright© 1996, 2004, 2007, 2013 by Tyndale House Foundation. Used by permission of Tyndale House Publishers Inc., Carol Stream, Illinois 60188. All rights reserved.)

*Some names and identifying details have been changed to protect the privacy of individuals.*

Cataloguing in Publication Data:
Title: Wisdom For Family Living
ISBN: 978-1-7637394-1-3  (pbk)
Subjects: FAM038000   FAMILY & RELATIONSHIPS / Reference; REL012030   RELIGION / Christian Living / Family & Relationships; REL011000   RELIGION / Christian Education / General

Design by initiateagency.com

# ACKNOWLEDGEMENTS

I would like to especially acknowledge my daughter Carolyn. Thank you for your assistance with technology and editing. I also want to thank my family members and friends who have written Forewords for the book and all those who have assisted with ideas, words, and wisdom even when you were unaware of it.

# DEDICATION

To my parents, Norman and Doreen Watson,
and
My parents-in-law, Jack and Jean Barrie.

These words are true of both mine
and my husband's homes.

*"Our home was a place of love and security always.
We taught our children to always put God first.
We set the example to love one another constantly.
This was foremost in our marriage for sixty years."*
Jean.

# CONTENTS

*Introduction* ..................................................... xi

*Wisdom in Marriage* ............................................1

*Wise Words for Men and Women* .....................37

*Wisdom in the Family* ........................................53

*Wisdom in Parenting* .........................................75

*Wisdom with Finances* ................................... 119

# INTRODUCTION

When we think about wisdom, its meaning, and how we can attain it, we need to go to Chapter 28 of the Book of Job. Here is what this man of God said to his friends after reasoning with them.

*"Where can wisdom be found?*
*Where does understanding dwell?*

*No mortal comprehends its worth; it cannot*
*be found in the land of the living.*
*It cannot be bought with the finest gold, nor*
*can its price be weighed out in silver.*
*Coral and jasper are not worthy of mention;*
*the price of wisdom is beyond rubies.*
*It cannot be bought with pure gold.*
*Where then does wisdom come from?*
*Where does understanding dwell?*
*It is hidden from the eyes of every living thing.*

*God understands the way to it and he
alone knows where it dwells,
for he views the ends of the earth and sees
everything under the heavens.*

*When he established the force of the wind
and measured out the waters,
when he made a decree for the rain and
a path for the thunderstorm,
then he looked at wisdom and appraised
it; he confirmed it and tested it.*

*And he said to the human race,
"THE FEAR OF THE LORD—that is WISDOM,
and TO SHUN EVIL IS UNDERSTANDING." NIV.*

There are days when all of us wish we had more wisdom to know how to handle the situation we face, to have the right words to put into a message or email, to know what to do to have a better marriage or discipline our children. Regardless of the situation or circumstance, we all experience a need to have more wisdom. Today, more than ever, we need more than the wisdom the world offers; we need to draw upon the divine wisdom God provides for each of us. James tells us, *"The wisdom that comes from heaven is first of all pure; then peace-loving, considerate, submissive, full of mercy and good fruit, impartial and sincere."* (James 3:17)

# INTRODUCTION

Most who read these words know of King Solomon's great wisdom, but have we genuinely taken his God-given wisdom and put it into practice in our everyday lives? In the following chapters, I have endeavoured to express some of God's wisdom through my experiences and observations to help you live more successfully as a family.

We have the power to improve our world to be a better place, but we must ask ourselves if we genuinely care. The reality is that our actions and attitudes profoundly impact our families, friends and the world around us.

I have always been fascinated with the growth of trees. Over many years, I have concluded that when they grow in proximity, they protect each other from the storms and tempests. The tree that stands alone is often the one that will be damaged or blown over in a storm. In contrast, a grove or group of trees that stand together will break the force of the same storm to protect each other, because their roots intertwine with the trees around them, helping to keep them upright and strong. Likewise, if we are to be protected from worldly influences, we need each other's support and understanding.

Even though technology has made our busy lives more effortless, we appear to be spinning faster than ever before, often wondering where time has gone and feeling out of our depth to cope with the pressures of life. Today, more than ever before, the thing that suffers most is our relationship with others, especially our relationships within our families.

The very roots of our lives are being eroded as we look at the increase in divorce rates, the lack of respect for one another in the home and the workplace, the disrespect of our children, the increase in juvenile crime, the indignity of parenthood and the distinctive differences between men and women.

When God told Solomon to ask for whatever he wanted, Solomon humbly asked for wisdom and understanding to rule over the Kingdom of Israel. 2 Chronicles 1:10-12, *"Give me wisdom and knowledge, that I may lead this people, for who is able to govern this great people of yours?"*

*God said to Solomon, "Since this is your heart's desire and you have not asked for wealth, possessions or honour, nor for the death of your enemies, and since you have not asked for a long life but for wisdom and knowledge to govern my people over whom I have made you king, therefore wisdom and knowledge will be given you."*

Today, with technology, we have so much information around us, which sometimes can be very confusing because **even though knowledge is beneficial, it is not wisdom**. We may possess vast knowledge with deep insight, yet we still struggle to prevent the pain that we continually inflict on one another and have no idea what makes us stumble again and again.

This is why we need God's wisdom, which teaches us how to use our knowledge. In Proverbs 4: 5-6, we read, *"Get wisdom, get understanding; do not forget my words or turn away from*

## INTRODUCTION

*them. Do not forsake wisdom, and she will protect you; love her, and she will watch over you."* Today, we are flooded with knowledge and technology, but we need God's wisdom to teach us how to live at peace with each other.

Wisdom is received through careful application of the Word of God to our lives. Asking for God's wisdom can bring remarkable changes to our everyday enjoyment of life. James 1:5 tells us, *"If any of you lacks wisdom, you should ask God, who gives generously to all without finding fault, and it will be given to you."* Often, wisdom can be as simple as a bit of common sense and consideration for each other.

Proverbs 12:15 says, *"The way of fools seems right to them, but the wise listen to advice."* During the American Civil War, President Abraham Lincoln wanted to please a politician, so he commanded the transfer of certain Union Army regiments. Upon receiving this order, the secretary of war, Edwin Stanton, refused to carry it out, proclaiming that the President was a fool. When Lincoln was told, he replied, *"If Stanton said that I'm a fool, then I must be because he is nearly always right, but I'll see for myself."* As they talked, the president realized his decision was a mistake and withdrew his command. Even though Stanton had called the President a fool, Lincoln was wise enough not to dig in his heels when he disagreed. Instead, **he listened to advice**, considered it, and changed his command.

There are two kinds of wisdom: 'earthly' and 'heavenly.' Earthly wisdom is marked by selfish ambition and disorder, endeavouring to put ourselves first. On the other hand, Heavenly wisdom is marked by humility, submission, and peacemaking. It is achieved by choosing to put others first, which leads to humility. James 3:13-15, *"Who is wise and understanding among you? Let them show it by their good life, by deeds done in the humility that comes from wisdom. But if you harbour bitter envy and selfish ambition in your hearts, do not boast about it or deny the truth. Such "wisdom" does not come down from heaven but is earthly, unspiritual, demonic."* **The two main factors determining the outcome of our lives' are how we think and our attitude to every situation.**

Both of these facts determine our habits and behaviour. These have been influenced by our past lives and all the information we have accumulated over the years. For instance, we all have personal views on disciplining our children, marriage, the government, the economy, education, work, and many other things. How we think and our attitude to how we respond can damage our lives and the lives of others far more than any of the challenges we face.

Life is challenging for everyone. We all face problems, which, when faced with the right attitude, can make us better, more responsible, and more likeable people. **An attitude of judgement and hate can ruin your relationship with others while simultaneously causing harm to yourself.** Holding a grudge or harbouring hate makes it difficult for others to be around us, and ultimately, it becomes challenging for us to live with ourselves as well.

Even if you are suffering or have deeply suffered, you can be a blessing to yourself and everyone around you by being kind. A smile is infectious; every breath is a gift, and your life will be beautiful if you allow it to be.

**Don't chase after happiness; instead, focus on being kind, and happiness will naturally follow**. Kindness begins with you. Never forget that there is hope and that the God of the Universe loves you more than you will ever understand.

I would suggest that the ideas in this book are not the only life-changing ideas that will help you; indeed, there are many, and no one can master every aspect of life. I have endeavoured to write to be practical and easy to understand, although it may not always be as easy to put into practice. This is where you must allow the words to inspire, encourage, reassure and give hope to the situation you are presently experiencing.

I am not the master of wisdom, nor would I be so presumptuous as to suggest that you will find all the answers you seek within these pages.

However, I encourage you to journal, making notes as you endeavour to make changes, so you can look back at the progress and be blessed by your achievements. We are told that forming a new habit only takes 21 days.

I have provided a page at the end of each section for your reflections to enable you to write your list of the principles that will make a difference for you.

Rather than trying to implement everything simultaneously, focus on mastering one principle at a time. This approach will help you elevate your life to a more harmonious place.

I pray that the following words will give your life blessing and joy every day.

# CHAPTER 1

# Wisdom in Marriage

Martin Luther beautifully expressed, *'There is no more lovely, friendly or charming relationship, communion or company than a good marriage.'* This sentiment should inspire us all to strive for the joy and fulfilment that a successful marriage can bring.

When two individuals share the same beliefs and values, they are better equipped to withstand challenges, maintain unity, and avoid the pitfalls of worldly philosophies. With God as the third entity in your marriage, your marriage will gain purpose and significance, as Ecclesiastes 4:12 reminds us, *"Though one may be overpowered, two can defend themselves."*

Today, we see beautiful, exquisite homes with spectacular gardens, but an extreme difference exists between a lovely house and a peaceful and happy home. We can admire a family or a home, but we are all aware that none of us knows what happens behind closed doors. Often, when on a plane, I have looked down on a country house that looked like a dot on the landscape and wondered who lived there. Whether they have had a happy and enjoyable family life surrounded by love and happiness or if the pressures of life have affected their lives.

Marriage is, without a doubt, the most complex and intimate human relationship. While achieving a perfect marriage is challenging—given that none of us are flawless—unfortunately, in many marriages, there is emotional distance and the relationship becomes muted, as though they are divorced psychologically, though not legally.

Studies estimate that around seventy-five percent of couples consider their relationship a failure, often masking their unhappiness behind a façade of contentment for the outside world. However, when you both contribute to creating and nurturing an environment filled with peace and harmony, you will have a truly fulfilled marriage, where **each is committed to making their partner the centre of their world instead of focusing on their own happiness** while simultaneously being committed to your children's upbringing.

Sometimes, when a partner feels overwhelmed and unsure of how to cope, they might seek advice from a friend and, without fully considering the long-term implications, make a hasty decision to leave. This can lead to significant challenges and a lonely experience, especially when raising children alone. Later, it can be disheartening to see that the advisor, who may still be happily married, might not have fully grasped the weight of the burden you had to shoulder. It's important to make decisions with careful consideration of their lasting impact on both your future and your family's well-being.

**God calls us to love and communicate with each other** to resolve our difficulties and maintain our commitment to each other rather than take what at the time seems the easy way out. As you do this, you become one in the flesh while still being two individuals with your own quirks and different opinions.

When your relationship as a married couple begins, and you become one, you are still two individuals with your ideas and different opinions, which, as individuals, each is entitled to. **Neither has the right to destroy this in their partner**. The relationship in a marriage should be an opportunity for each to grow as you show love and trust to each other.

We often want to change and fix our spouse when it might be more beneficial to turn our attention inward and work on improving ourselves. **Recognising our own needs and weaknesses can foster a healing environment** that brings love, acceptance, safety, and intimacy, allowing both to value each other and grow physically and spiritually together. (1 Peter 3:1-7).

When you make your partner the centre of your world, your love will grow and flourish. If your partner does something that bothers or annoys you, pray about it rather than addressing it directly, because God is the only one who can change a person, and He might reveal areas where you need to adjust your own perspective or behaviour. Often, when we are open to change within ourselves, we find that the changes we hope for in our partner will occur naturally, without confrontation. **Embrace prayer over criticism,** and watch your relationship be transformed.

Why do so many marriages fail? It can often stem from a mindset focused on receiving rather than giving. Make the decision today and choose to say in your soul, **"Let it begin with me."** A married couple needs to consistently feel love for each other. In a Christian marriage, we need to uplift and disciple one another in love and grow together in faith. Take the attitude of **'I will work on me for you if you work on you for me.'**

Nancy Mayer once said**,** *"Marriage is a process, a fluid relationship that assumes many different forms over the years, a relationship that is always either growing or deteriorating."*

Money can cause tension in a marriage, so I encourage you to openly discuss your money and debts together to create a clear plan to bring you financial peace and freedom. (I'll delve deeper into this later in the Chapter on Wisdom with Finances) By addressing your money issues together, you ensure transparency and build trust. Value your income (your most significant asset) while avoiding a mindset of what I earn is mine. To maintain trust and avoid misunderstandings, you should always discuss the purchase of substantial investments together. Most importantly, remember that your finances are a blessing from God, and He wants us to be generous. Honour Him first by giving a portion of your income to Him, and you will find that your needs will always be met.

Even though we all desire good health, health challenges can put significant pressure on a marriage, causing pain and financial burdens. While we have no control over this, we can take proactive steps to take good care of the body God entrusted to us. It's our responsibility to take good care of ourselves by eating nutritious foods, getting adequate sleep and staying active. **(avoid becoming couch potatoes).**

Wherever possible, prepare your meals at home rather than waste money on takeaway, even though it is nice to enjoy takeaway occasionally. Have an open mind to what is happening with your health, as God can change your thinking and show you what to do. Your body requires good nourishment and sleep to maintain good health.

Paul says in 1 Corinthians 6:19-20, *"Do you not know that your bodies are temples of the Holy Spirit, who is in you, whom you have received from God? You are not your own; you were bought at a price. Therefore, honour God with your bodies."*

In the years ahead of you, there will be many joyous occasions when you will laugh together and enjoy life to the fullest. There will also be challenging times when you will need the encouragement and support of each other to help you through. **Always uplift and show kindness to each other**; this is a special gift because as the years pass, it becomes very easy to notice your partner's faults instead of their virtues. **Instead, strive to see the qualities your Heavenly Father sees in your loved one,** making it easier to forgive each other and move forward together. The most incredible wealth we can show another is love, kindness and generosity. These acts of kindness will last longer than a lifetime.

As a married couple, **it's essential to adhere to the same principles you expect your partner to submit to.** No one should assume the position of authority by acting independently and expecting the other to comply. Each must accept and respect each other's boundaries.

When your marriage is inspired by **LOVE and COMMUNICATION**, making your partner the centre of your thoughts, care, and tenderness, your lives will be woven together in a deep and meaningful way. God created each of you to be free spirits and gave you the responsibility of being called to love Him and each other.

## _Building love into your marriage._

What is love – Love is the sovereign preference of one person for another. The well-known passage in the Bible makes it very clear.

> *"Love is – PATIENT. Love is - KIND.*
> *Love – DOES NOT ENVY.*
> *Love – DOES NOT BOAST.*
> *Love – IS NOT PROUD.*
> *Love – DOES NOT DISHONOUR OTHERS.*
> *Love – IS NOT SELF-SEEKING.*
> *Love – IS NOT EASILY ANGERED.*
> *Love – KEEPS NO RECORD OF WRONGS.*
> *Love – DOES NOT DELIGHT IN EVIL,*
> *but Love – REJOICES WITH THE TRUTH.*
> *It always protects, always trusts,*
> *always hopes, always perseveres."*
> (1 Corinthians 13:4-7.) NIV

You and your spouse both need this kind of love and are responsible for giving it to each other. You must love each other unconditionally while at the same time accepting and appreciating the love your partner extends to you without feeling that you are giving more than receiving. **As you give, so you will receive.**

Be cautious about idealizing your partner, as real people can never fully match our fantasies. Many, when they marry, bring their box of hopes, dreams, and desires, believing that they have the perfect vision for their relationship, only to find that too often, they become unrealistic expectations. Marriage isn't about fulfilling personal desires at the expense of your partner, it's about mutual support and understanding. Jesus gave us the example in John 13:34, *"A new command I give you: Love one another. As I have loved you, so you must love one another."* His example shows us that true love means uplifting our partner and striving to meet their needs.

No one is perfect, so don't expect more than your partner can give at that time. Focus on your own growth and embrace reality with your spouse, allowing them the time to grow through the love and support you offer. Both of you have needs and weaknesses, and a strong marriage is built on addressing what is, rather than what should be. Connect on a genuine, everyday level and **face each other's needs and weaknesses together.**

Quite often, we have high expectations of our partners when **what we need is an accepting nature**. When we accept our spouse as they are, it produces real change. Real love says, *'I love you, not for anything you do for me or how much you love me, but I love you for who you are—completely, sacrificially and unconditionally.'* Acceptance is necessary to feel valued, safe, and loved and to experience deep intimacy.

When you get frustrated about the person you chose to live with, reflect on how disagreeable you have been to God. **The** growth of love in your marriage stops when you focus on finding fault and allow frustration to take over.

Both human and divine love needs to be nurtured to endure.

## Importance of Acceptance

- We need to see our partner's uniqueness and worth before God.

- Just as God is willing to accept us because He loves us, so the acceptance of our partner reveals our love for them. **Change in them must come from God.**

- Through acceptance, we build self-worth.

- Acceptance sees the other person's value to the relationship.

- Acceptance brings peace of mind and motivates change.

- Acceptance means forgiveness. *'Love does not demand change; it produces it.'*

## Areas of acceptance

- **Respect** is vital to loving your partner. Respect them for who they are, and the respect and trust in each other will grow. Always show them respect by being polite to them. **Avoid telling each other what to do all the time.**

- **Family.** Each must respect their partner's family background and try to see the good in them.

- **Habits.** Sometimes, this can be difficult but choose the words and time to speak about this carefully.

- **Appearance.** If we like our partners to look their best by dressing smartly, we must do the same for them by presenting ourselves well.

- **Vocation.** Don't expect or pressure your partner to be or do something that is not their field of expertise and enjoyment.

- **Temperament.** We all have different personalities; the important thing is that we have a Spirit-controlled temperament, which is God's work – not ours.

- **Spiritual life.** Sometimes, we might feel that our partner's spiritual journey differs from our own, which can lead to subtle criticism. Instead of expressing these feelings, focus on supporting them through prayer by handing it over to God. Remember, we all grow spiritually in our own unique way.

## Steps to Acceptance

- Remember, God has placed you together, and your temperaments and abilities can often complement each other. Try to see your partner's value and show appreciation by expressing it to each other. **Never let romance leave your marriage.**

- Acceptance is our responsibility. **Don't keep pointing out your partner's faults by nagging and whinging at them, but rather focus on prayer.** Sometimes, it's through personal reflection and growth that we become better equipped to support change in our partner. Trust that God will guide you through your own transformation. In Philippians 2, Paul tells us about having the right attitude, and in verse 14, we read, *"Do everything without complaining or arguing."*

- Think before you speak. Paul warned us about unwholesome talk in Ephesians 4:29, *"Do not let any unwholesome talk come out of your mouths, but only what is helpful for building others up according to their needs, that it may benefit those who listen."* Often, **it's not what we say but how we say it that hurts**. When we speak harshly and deny our partner's point of view, it can quickly destroy decency and compassion in the relationship.

- Admit when you are wrong and ask forgiveness. **Always be willing to forgive each other.** Be big enough to be the first to say sorry. **Forgiveness has a powerful effect on both parties, moving you toward healing and reconciliation**. *"Bear with each other and forgive one* another .... *Forgive as the Lord forgave you."* (Colossians 3:13)

- When you have an issue, try to understand your partner's point of view. Commit it to God to work out and wait for His help. **Take courage when things go wrong; if possible, pray about it together.**

- **True love is about giving selflessly, without expecting anything in return.** When a person is motivated to give just to receive something in return, this could be a sign of manipulation rather than genuine love. *"Dear children, let us not love with words or speech but with actions and in truth."* 1John 3:18.

- The past cannot be altered, so it's important to accept what has happened and focus on moving forward together. Suffering and challenges are part of life, enriching our ability to connect deeply with others. **True happiness isn't about being free from problems but developing the resilience to cope with and rise above them.** Remember, *'A diamond shines most against black velvet.'* If you have been hurt somehow, choose the time wisely to let your partner know of your hurt without labouring the point.

- Understand that some need more sleep than others to sustain their physical strength, which can also be influenced by diet. As a couple, it's important to **prioritize** a healthy diet and ensure you both get adequate rest to support your overall well-being.

- **Take your problems to the Lord** individually or, preferably, together as a couple. Trust God to resolve them according to His will and promises. Psalm 55:22 says, *"Cast your cares on the Lord and he will sustain you; he will never let the righteous be shaken."* **Ask God for wisdom, revelation, and understanding each day.**

## LOVE ADVICE

Keep your love stronger than your hate or anger. Say 'I love you' often.

It is better to bend a little than to break (There can be wisdom in compromise)

Always believe in the best of your partner. (Doubt is the enemy of imagination)

Keep your opinion of your partner high, and they will live up to it.

True friendship is the basis for a lasting relationship

Be more courteous and kinder to your partner than to any friend.

Sometimes in life, we only need a hug to make it right

Stay in love. True love is about giving. Too many marriages are based on conditional love – I love you because, or – I love you if you do.

Thank your Lord daily for your spouse and all they do to bring you happiness.

Be aware of becoming a controlling partner.

Be big enough and first to say 'I'm sorry' when you disagree.

*"And above all, you must be loving, for love is the link to the perfect life."* Colossians 3:14 (Moffatt)

**Meditate:** Reflect on the outstanding moments of love in your life.

# **REFLECTIONS**

## *The Physical Intimacy of Marriage*

It is incredible how many couples are unaware of how vital a healthy sexual relationship should be. There should be freedom in the sexual relationship, as the result will bring a more fulfilled and enjoyable experience for both. Each should feel free to discuss their needs and desires with their partner. As individuals, seek new ways to please your spouse so that each enjoys the completeness of the experience.

There is a big difference between men and women in the sexual relationship. Men are more visually stimulated, and women are more responsive to touch. A healthy sexual relationship is a crucial part of the marriage relationship, as it provides security, happiness and self-confidence. It also plays a key role in creating a strong bond within family life.

A woman's natural response to her partner is affected by how she feels and values his tender protection and being truly loved by him. Her response will come from his touch and desire to make his spouse feel fulfilled. God's intention for sexual intercourse was that in the climax, the two become one in a highly complex mental process. If you are newly married, give yourselves time to understand and get to know each other emotionally and physically so that, over time, you will find a uniqueness in your relationship together.

Likewise, it's also important for the woman to be aware of a man's strong desire for his wife to give herself to him. Take time to make yourself appealing so that both enjoy the experience. Have a positive attitude to your sexual relationship so you both appreciate and enjoy it. Remember, intimacy is a vital part of the marriage relationship and reflects God's design for marital connection.

A man must show pure love to his wife, protecting her from harm and providing for her desire to feel care and tenderness. Be aware that the expressions of love toward each other change as time passes. Both partners should cultivate an unbreakable commitment to each other and God, a bond that remains steadfast throughout their lives until death.

Outside of marriage, sex is a counterfeit relationship in which abiding satisfaction is exchanged for immediate gratification, and sometimes, the beauty and lasting worth of a God-designed intimacy is sacrificed for an inappropriate and fleeting encounter that perverts the perfect plan of God. Within a marriage, sexual intercourse should be a strong natural desire for each other, being a special time for both. Take time to read the 'Song of Songs' in the Bible together, where you will find that sexual intimacy is good, powerful, life-giving, and unifying in a unique and meaningful way, bringing marital bliss and physical intimacy.

In 1 Cor.7:3-5, Paul speaks to the early church about the importance of the relationship between a man and his wife.

*"The husband should fulfil his marital duty to his wife, and likewise the wife to her husband.*

*The wife does not have authority over her own body but yields it to her husband. In the same way, the husband does not have authority over his own body but yields it to his wife.*

*Do not deprive each other except perhaps by mutual consent and for a time, so that you may devote yourselves to prayer. Then come together again so that Satan will not tempt you because of your lack of self-control."*

When a man or woman knows and experiences the satisfaction of a healthy sexual relationship at home, there will be no desire to seek satisfaction elsewhere.

*"Be kind to one another, forgiving one another."* Ephesians 4:32.

**Meditate:** It is a unity of soul as well as body.

# **REFLECTIONS**

## *Building Communication*

*Words are, of course, the most powerful drug used by mankind*
Rudyard Kipling.

Communication is not just talking but endeavouring to understand your partner, listening to what they are saying and trying to understand their point of view.

When you think differently about the issues that arise, have the confidence to pray together, and individually, about your differences, asking God to make the way very clear to you both. I am increasingly convinced that the most significant thing a Christian couple can do each day is to read God's Word and pray together, for it is the basis of God's plan for your marriage. If your partner is not open to praying, know that God understands and is still in control. Pray for the situation yourself, being mindful not to pray in front of your partner. Instead, find time to spend and connect with God alone.

## Communication skills

- Be mindful not to have a more spiritual attitude than your partner, as it may make them feel spiritually inferior, causing them to feel unable to measure up to your level.

- Develop common interests that you can do together. Always support your partner in the interests they enjoy. From time to time, go on a date night together.

- Encourage each other by being sensitive to each other's needs and speaking words of encouragement and kindness. Tell your partner how much you appreciate them and **thank them** when they help you. **When was the last time you spoke a word of encouragement to your spouse?**

- Be interested in what is going on in the world around you.

- Make an effort to keep yourself looking attractive and appealing so your partner remains attracted to you and not someone else, even in seemingly innocent situations. This communicates love to your spouse.

- Men, a woman likes her man to be clean and neatly dressed, and women, your man likes to feel proud to call you, his wife.

- Cultivate your love life by occasionally buying some small gift to tell them they are special to you. **TELL YOUR PARTNER EVERY DAY THAT YOU LOVE THEM.**

- The golden rule for relationship building. - **Always be willing to say I'm sorry first**, being genuine and willing to forgive. - Let your spouse know that you appreciate them by being sensitive to the fact that they are hurting. Avoid saying sorry and then immediately tell them you love them. **ALWAYS BE TRUTHFUL AND GENUINE IN WHAT YOU SAY.**

- Make sure you cultivate a home, not a house. Let it be where every family member wants to spend time because they know there is love and understanding for them there. A place where they are comfortable to bring their friends and not just somewhere to sleep and eat.
  A home should be where each one feels they want to be and can relax without pressure.

- **Don't kill your communication** with outbursts of anger, long periods of silence, or ignoring the other person. These behaviours will harm you, not build your relationship, and you will achieve nothing. Women try to keep the tears at bay, as many men find it challenging to cope with them.
  Say what you want in a civilised manner, or better still, wait until both have settled down and then talk as mature adults. If your partner doesn't like tears and you need to cry, step away and process your emotions.

- If you have something to talk about with your partner, choose wisely the time to do so. Never confront them with it when they arrive home from work unless it is an emergency. A calm and relaxed moment can lead to a more meaningful conversation.

- Take a moment to greet each other when you come together after work. If possible, relax with a coffee or tea and spend a few minutes hearing about the other person's day, then pursue what needs to be done on the home level. **'Let the wife make the husband glad to come home, and let the husband make his wife sorry to see him leave.'** Martin Luther.

- Don't be lazy. Always do your part in the relationship and home to make things flow with appreciation for each other.

Communication involves talking, timing, and being sensitive to your partner, so look carefully at what will improve your communication and take the necessary action.

## COMMUNICATION ADVICE

- **Avoid multitasking** – Focus entirely on your partner when you're having a conversation.

- **Stay Humble:** Do not express your opinions as if you have all the answers; no one is always correct.

- **Be honest:** Don't hesitate to admit when you don't know something.

- **Remember,** your communication is about both of you, not just yourself.

- **Ask Open-Ended Questions:** Use words like "how," "when," "where," and "why" to encourage discussion; avoid telling, as it comes across as bossy.

- **Be Concise:** Keep your points brief and avoid repeating yourself.

- **Give Your Full Attention:** Ensure you are fully present and give attention to your partner during a conversation.

- **LISTEN -** Be interested in what your partner is saying. Keep your mouth closed and your ears open. Avoid criticizing, insulting or making fun of your partner.

  **Proverbs 20 tells us –**

  a. Wine produces mockers; alcohol leads to brawls. Those led astray by drink cannot be wise.

  b. To avoid a fight is a mark of honour.

  c. Those too lazy to plough (work) in the right season will have no food at the harvest. NLT.

- **Criticism:** Be aware of criticising your partner when they are driving, knowing that you would not appreciate their criticism of you.

*"Through patience, a ruler can be persuaded, and a gentle tongue can break a bone."* Proverbs 25:15.

**Meditate:** What qualities constitute a team spirit?

## **REFLECTIONS**

## *Key Values of a Good Marriage*

- If you desire a genuinely loving and stable marriage, then both must follow God's design, where the husband takes the leadership role. Ephesians 5:23 clarifies that a man has responsibility for leadership in his home, and the wife is to respect that role. **When the man leads (not demands), the wife will respect her husband's leadership, which instinctively builds love within the man for his wife, resulting in God's design of leadership, respect and love.**

- For a marriage to be happy and prosperous, the husband and wife must be committed to loving each other unconditionally. **Whoever we value, we honour.**

- As a spouse, always try to be available when needed. If possible, stop what you are doing and help your spouse.

- Spend valued time together (without children) every day. Don't be on the phone and don't spend this time talking with a friend. Also, don't spend this valued time just talking about the children. Learn to listen to each other. (2 ears and one mouth) *"Everyone should be quick to listen, slow to speak and slow to become angry."* (James 1:19)

- **Support each other by not just putting things down but PUTTING THEM AWAY.** This action will always be appreciated. (This good habit will save many arguments)

- **If something needs doing, DO IT,** even when you think it is your partner's turn or responsibility. Once it's done, you will feel uplifted, and you can relax together. We need to do what needs to be done simply because it's the right thing to do.

  There were four people. *One day, there was an important job that needed to be done, but nobody did it because they all thought that somebody would. It ended up with everybody blaming somebody, and nobody did what anybody could have done.* **Just do it.**

- **Give as opposed to receive**—Don't expect anything. Read Ephesians 5:25-33. God shows us that love is thoughtful and tender. In a happy, fulfilled marriage, we must love each other and follow Christ's example.

  When we make our partner the centre of our lives and willingly give ourselves to them without thinking about what's in it for me, their response will be to respond similarly to you. **Expectations can damage a relationship.**

- **Pray instead of saying.** At times of disagreement, choose your words carefully so you don't say something you will regret. Choose words that will encourage because gentle words bring life and health. (Prov. 9:13) **Avoid the words 'you always' and 'you never,' as they will demoralize.**

- **Deal with your anger.** - Be the bigger person who has the courage to say 'sorry' first. *"Do not let the sun go* *down on your anger and give no opportunity to the devil"* (Ephesians 4:26-27). God blesses a marriage where each spouse is willing to apologize. It's time to kiss and make up.

- **Hurt can make you bitter** - Eph 4:29-32. Don't let bitterness and hurt destroy your marriage. At some stage in any relationship, there will be hurt. Apologize quickly. If you harbour hurt, it will only destroy you. Ask God to help you overcome and give His peace to you.

- Read and know what's happening around you and develop new friends.

- **Don't wallow in self-pity,** or you will destroy both yourself and those within your family. Replace it with a positive attitude and bring it to God. He told us what to do in Phil.4:6-7, *"Do not be anxious about anything, but in every situation, by prayer and petition, with thanksgiving, present your requests to God. And the peace of God, which transcends all understanding, will guard your hearts and your minds in Christ Jesus."*

- You cannot change what has happened, but you can change the future by changing your attitude. **IF YOU WANT A BETTER MARRIAGE, THEN BECOME A BETTER SPOUSE.**

- **Appreciate your partner and say something uplifting every day.** Arguing, demanding and yelling only show your bad attitude and that you do not respect or value your spouse.

## *Maturity in Marriage*

Marriages don't break down overnight; it is often the constant finding of fault, nagging, and complaining that gradually wear away the relationship to where one or the other can no longer put up with it. We must remember that none of us are perfect, and we all do things that annoy our spouses. **Look for something to compliment your spouse on each day to build their self-esteem**. Something like a tidy house or a hard day's work. Very soon, you will find that they, in return, will think about what they can do to make your life better.

Too often, men feel that their wives don't understand their workload, and the wives feel they are not appreciated for all they do in the home and for their husbands and children.

Marriages can suffer because of immaturity. We need to get over issues like toothpaste tubes, toilet seats and taking out the garbage. **Just do it,** and gradually, you may notice positive changes. If things don't change, then be mature enough not to let it bother you.

Devotion (LOVE) – Be devoted to each other by investing quality time with each other and the Lord. When God is the centre of your marriage, the closer you are to the hub (God) of a wheel, the closer you will be to each other and your children.

Discussion (COMMUNICATION) – Communicate with each other and your children. Discuss your plans and problems together, not necessarily at the meal table (keep mealtime happy).

If your health is causing you physical and emotional distress, share your needs with your partner before anyone else, and pray about it together.

Be focused together, and **do not allow anything or anyone to disrupt your home and family life**. Plan your lives together and set goals–holidays, outings and time together. Practise the discipline of not wanting to have the last word. If you fail to plan, you plan to fail.

**Operate on sound financial policies.** Keep expenses less than your income. Poor money management can cause stress and tension and quickly erode your relationship and home life. Make it a priority to discuss your finances and budget together and remember that **material things do not bring true happiness.**

**Instant gratification is the sale of today.** Don't want everything overnight. Be cautious about taking on too many loans and credit cards. If you can't afford it, wait and then you will appreciate it more. If you plan your finances together and stick to your budget, it will be a blessing. A budget doesn't limit your spending; it defines it, and you know where your money is going and what you can spend. Aim to stay out of debt.

**Overcome conflict.** When two individuals come together in a relationship, each is unique in their thinking, likes, and dislikes, so differences of opinion are inevitable. It is like two rivers merging into one, turbulence occurs, but steadily, it settles to become a stronger force. **Your relationship is not just about you.**

The secret is to listen carefully (James 1:19) to your partner. Replace accusations and insults with listening and understanding. Try to see the other person's point of view as well as help them to understand how you feel.

Always select a suitable time to talk about your differences in a civilized manner. Pray together about it, for prayer has the power to transform even the most challenging situations. Don't allow the problem to come between you. Your partner may not want to pray together, so pray about it yourself, asking God to resolve the situation. If you are wrong, be big enough to apologize and make up.

Resolve your conflict, and don't allow it to harm your relationship; instead, use it to draw you closer together.

**One of the greatest gifts we have is self-control.** If we spent more time thinking about the circumstances of our conflict, we would be able to control our lives and feelings more. Sometimes, an out-of-control action creates a situation where other things spin out of control, and our feelings and emotions are affected. Decide on your standards. **Often, all it takes is to embrace each other, showing an act of acceptance.**

MAKE CHRIST THE CENTRE OF YOUR RELATIONSHIP.

A good relationship will only improve with Christ at the centre of your marriage as you allow Him to be your leader.

In John's Gospel, we read about Jesus turning the water into wine. This was important in many ways, but Mary's instruction to the servants says it all: *"Whatever He (Jesus) says unto you to do, do it."* This is the wisdom we need for a marriage relationship of peace and happiness that God intended for us.

**Integrity** in your marriage is crucial, and you are the only one who can maintain it.

- IF YOU WANT A BETTER MARRIAGE, BECOME A BETTER SPOUSE
- IT IS BETTER TO TRUST GOD THAN TO ENJOY LIFE
- THE SECRET IS TO MAKE THE OTHER PERSON'S LIFE BETTER EVERY DAY
- BE FRIENDS AND EQUALS BEFORE ANYTHING ELSE
- LIVE EACH DAY IN THE MOMENT; YOU CAN'T CHANGE THE PAST, SO ENJOY YOUR MARRIED LIFE TODAY TO THE FULLEST.

- WHEN YOU TRUST AND ANTICIPATE THE BEST OUTCOME, YOUR SPOUSE WILL LIVE UP TO YOUR EXPECTATIONS.

- CONTROL AND INTIMACY ARE OPPOSITES.

- DON'T KEEP YOUR HEALTH ISSUES A SECRET FROM EACH OTHER.

- ATTACK YOUR PROBLEMS TOGETHER SO YOU DON'T ATTACK EACH OTHER.

- NEGATIVE THOUGHTS ALWAYS BRING JUDGMENT. TURN YOUR NEGATIVE THOUGHTS INTO PRAYER.

In a good marriage relationship, you will be in love with someone who respects you, loves you for who you are and understands you even in the madness and frustration of everyday life.

- Someone who wants to help you be a better you, who guides and supports you.

- Someone who still talks to you after conflict.

- Someone who misses you and wants to be with you more than anyone else.

## *Marriage Advice from 1886*

*Let your love be stronger than your hate or anger.
Learn the wisdom of compromise, for it is
better to bend a little than to break.
Believe the best rather than the worst.
People have a way of living up or down
to your opinion of them.
Remember that true friendship is the basis for any lasting
relationship. The person you choose to marry is deserving
of the courtesies and kindnesses you give to your friends.
The more things change the more they are the same.*

Jane Wells (1866)

## **REFLECTIONS**

CHAPTER TWO

# Wise Words for Men and Women

## MEN – THE LOVERS AND LEADERS

*"Husbands, in the same way, be considerate as you live with your wives, and treat them with respect as the weaker partner and as heirs with you of the gracious gift of life, so that nothing will hinder your prayers."* (1 Peter 3:7)

Today, there is a great need for men to take their God-given leadership roles within the marriage, home, and especially in the spiritual leadership of their families. The Apostle Paul refers to the fact that just as Christ is head of the church, the husband is called to be the head of his wife and family.

**Men ask yourselves:** 'Am I taking the courage given me by God and leading my wife and children or am I leaving this to my wife.?'

Our amazing, glorious God created man in his image. In Exodus 15:2-3, we witness God's might as he overthrows the Egyptians at the Red Sea. God grants Moses and the Israelites victory, and they sing His praise. *"The Lord is my strength and song, and he is become my salvation: he is my God, my father's God, and I will exalt him. The Lord is a man of war: the Lord is his name."* God desires men to mirror His strength, to rise up, to be courageous, and to take control by loving and caring for their partners and children, and to live out their lives in the image of the mighty God who created them.

Men, don't just go along with whatever your partner wants in order to keep the peace; in doing this, you are not the head of your home. **This is the time for communication and love to occur with each other and before God.** Ask God to show both of you what needs to happen to give the best outcome for your family.

A woman wants a man willing to defend and fight for her, and women want to reveal their beauty to a courageous, masculine man.

Men, in general, regard God as distant or weak (this often results from their earthly father). **What is your image of God**

**like?** Do you have a picture of someone who is meek and mild or a nice guy, when He is the opposite?

Men who are burdened by their fathers' wounds must learn from God and be like Him. You may not be able to change the wound given by your father, but you can seek God's forgiveness for both you and your father. This act of forgiveness is not just a step, but a leap towards finding direction to a happier life.

**A spiritual life with direction and purpose begins when we accept our hurts.** An unforgiving or bitter heart will destroy your life and the lives of your spouse and family. *"Let all bitterness, and wrath, and anger, and clamour, and evil speaking, be put away from you, with all malice."* Eph. 4:31.

To become the person God wants you to be, you must discipline yourself to spend time every day in the Lord's presence. **This time with God is not just necessary but crucial for your survival in the battle of life.**

**Imagine if this was your only way to survive; I am sure you would find a way to make this time with God your priority.**

Guide your family and have special times with your children. Play, wrestle with your boys, and have prayer and snuggle time when they go to bed. These moments of togetherness are not only important, but they also bring joy and warmth to your family life.

Even though your partner may not admit or realize it, the security you give her is essential to her well-being. Many women don't realize this until their husbands have passed away or left. Having the security of a good man gives a woman a feeling of peace.

In his commentary on Ephesians, William Hendriksen writes, *'He is her head as being vitally interested in her welfare.'*

If your family is to survive today's stresses and dangers, husbands and fathers, it will be because you have provided loving spiritual leadership in your home.

The bond between parents and children and your family's security will largely depend on the bond between the parents. The better the parents' relationship of oneness and love, the greater the security the children will feel.

**As a husband and father, the most significant thing you can do for your children is love and care for their mother.**

Let your children see your love and affection for your wife. When children experience love between their parents, they will feel part of a strong and satisfying bond within the family.

Children learn how to express love as they watch their parents interact and express their love for each other.

Share the responsibilities of the home, especially if your wife works.

Work as a team so that either of you can do anything for your family.

After a day's work, your responsibility is being at home with your family. Other times can be spent with your mates. Don't come home from work and chill, expecting your wife to wait on you.

Be clean and dress neatly so your wife wants to be seen with you.

The husband is responsible for leading his family into God's presence by leading them in family prayer and praying with them at meals and during the day.

You should **prioritize regular church attendance for your family**, showing them the importance of meeting for worship with God's family.

### Issues to consider.

- Do not let your relationship lack tenderness, politeness and sociability. Women want to know and feel loved and fought for.

- Understanding your wife's temperament will enable a better relationship.

- Always be honest and truthful, especially in financial matters.

- Don't make snide remarks about your wife or criticize her in front of others.
- Take time to be a good listener without judging or presuming.
- Don't say hurtful things like; you're just like your mother, you're always in a bad mood, you don't think, what's wrong with you, stop complaining. Take time to list things you say that are hurtful and replace each with positive encouragement.
- Accept the past and move on.
- Men always remember that your wife's most basic needs are,
    1. to experience your affection.
    2. to have time each day to be open and honest with each other.
    3. to know that you take your responsibility very seriously when it comes to financial support.
    4. to be committed to having a happy and contented life together.
- **Tell her you love her every day**, and occasionally buy her some flowers or chocolates.

- A woman needs to know that you genuinely love her and pursue her before she will let you experience her innermost being.

**God needs good, spiritual men to lead their families.**

*"Enjoy life with your wife, whom you love, all the days of this… life that God has given you under the sun."* Ecclesiastes 9:9.

<u>**Meditate:**</u> A plant wilts when we forget to 'cherish' it. Love is also sensitive to forgetfulness.

# REFLECTIONS

## WOMEN – GOD'S HOMEMAKERS

*"A wife of noble character who can find? She is worth far more than rubies. Her husband has full confidence in her and lacks nothing of value. She brings him good, not harm, all the days of her life."* (Proverbs 31:10-12)

The role of a wife and mother in our world, our churches, and especially our homes will only be strong and life-changing for those who live with her when she is devoted to a deep and meaningful relationship with the Lord God.

It is as though God has empowered women to be the standard that others will observe to build their own lives. Unfortunately, many women today have let their standards drop, often because they have busy lives at home and work, resulting in little time for them to sit and enjoy the company of their husbands.

The mother is the spirit of the home, as everything revolves around her. I have always believed that this is why a wife and mother must maintain their standards; otherwise, the home is like an empty space in the family's life.

As the husband leads, **the wife has the power of influence,** which is a unique and great responsibility. Women, we are not here to overrule our partners. God has made your partner the head of the home and of you. You must listen, and if you disagree, you certainly have the right to say what you think. Discuss the matter together to reach a decision both are happy with.

In Ephesians 5:22-32, Paul gives a clear explanation of the role both the husband and wife need to follow to have a blessed marriage. God needs you to respect your husband's God-given role. **When a wife respects the role of her husband, her husband will grow spiritually to respect and love his wife more, which in turn will cause the effect of leadership, respect and love.**

Avoid taking the leadership role away from your husband, causing him to become weak, instead of leading his family. This is not to say that sometimes when the husband does not allow God's guidance in his role, a spirit-filled woman must step up and lead the family.

Ask yourself: **'Am I allowing my husband to lead me, or do I somehow stop him from taking his role?'**

**Times of conflict call for communication and prayer**, seeking God's will for the best outcome for your family. God does not want you to override your partner to the extent that he complies to keep the peace.

How many great men and women have come from a family where the mother influenced their lives? Winston Churchill once said, *"The greatest of all my teachers was my mother."*

When a man loses his wife, he often finds it especially hard to move forward. His home is empty without the love and companionship of a wife of many years.

Women, you have a special place, a God-given role to stand with and beside your husband in life.

## Virtues of a good woman

**Be a beautiful person inside,** with a heart filled with the Holy Spirit, producing a calm, peaceful, warm and understanding woman. (1 Peter 3:4) **Beauty comes from a heart at rest.**

The true beauty of a woman is found within, **through a deep relationship with God**, and is related to having wisdom.

**Be attractive** – Every woman wants to be prettier, and millions of dollars are spent annually on the beauty industry. A courageous person once said, *"There are no ugly women, just lazy ones."* However, let us realize that being attractive to our partner takes on many aspects and does not mean we have to be extravagant with money.

**It is also important to your partner that you maintain your appearance.** Today, many women and men don't seem to care about how they look to other people.

Your appearance is important, for your partner will feel attracted to you and be proud of you. Many marriages have fallen apart because the husband was attracted to another woman's outward beauty.

The secret is to respect your appearance by wearing attractive clothes (not necessarily expensive), choosing a hairstyle and makeup to suit you, exercising, and maintaining good health through eating good nourishing food. *"For physical training is of some value, but godliness has value for all things, holding promise for both the present life and the life to come."* (1 Tim.4:8)

Don't forget that a man loves to come home to a home-cooked meal, not takeaway.

You cannot maintain the spirit of the home if you are sick and unwell. If you are unwell, seek professional help and consider taking some vitamins. **Most importantly, ask God for guidance as to what to do.** Throughout my life, I have often sought God's guidance with my health, and praise Him for the ways He has led and guided me.

**Your worth** – Accept yourself, for God made you unique, and no other woman is like you. Regardless of what anyone may say, you are unique, and if you are a child of God, then you are a Princess.

Please don't dwell on the negative; instead, discipline your mind to see the positive things, especially regarding your thoughts of your partner.

Do not allow the negative influence of soapies and novels to destroy the good, pure, and lovely things in your life. Too many relationships suffer from the materialistic, so-called perfect world displayed in movies and novels.

Develop a mental picture of a woman God calls to be filled with love, charm and dignity, and then you will gradually develop these qualities in your life.

Being able to laugh and be cheerful can defuse tension. Also, being able to laugh at yourself shows a person who understands her worth.

Take some time each day to be in a quiet place in God's presence, allowing Him to speak His wisdom into your life.

## Being an alluring lover

Ladies, God made you sexual, and He wants you to appreciate and enjoy it. After all, it was His idea to share your body, soul, and spirit with your husband, and only him.

A man likes his woman to be eager for him, not just willing to keep him happy.

It is important to a man that you are attractive and attracted to him. It is essential to his self-worth and prevents lust as opposed to love.

Be relaxed, refreshed (perfume helps), and adventurous in the garments you adorn yourself with before the act of sex. Admire his body, and don't make excuses. **Seduce him**.

Every woman wants to feel safe in the intimacy of sex. For some, it can be scary; you can feel vulnerable and completely naked in your soul and body, but God wants women to stop dominating and trust their husbands by offering their true selves.

Abuse will bring negative and guilty feelings to the relationship. In such an instance, you need to choose a time and seek honest communication with your partner and, where necessary, a counsellor. Although you may be emotionally scarred or hurt, endeavour to understand that God always forgives.

**Issues to consider.**

- Be a beautiful person inside and out.
- **Eat properly** - Good health is essential for beauty and vitality.
- **Exercise daily**—Exercise will help you sleep better. Even 5 minutes a day will make you feel better. A brisk walk works wonders, helping to clear your mind.
- Get Adequate sleep. Don't sit up late when you have to rise early the next day.
- **Learn to relax** - When you are relaxed, it will lighten your partner's attitude. *"A heart at peace gives life to the body."* (Prov.14:30)
- **Take a personal inventory** - Occasionally ask yourself, "Do I look my best? Are there ways I can improve my

*appearance? Is my hair and makeup becoming? Do I look fresh and well-groomed?"*

- Give to others, especially your partner. When you draw your strength from your loving Heavenly Father, your needs are met, and you will feel motivated to reach out confidently to give joy to others.

- Stop criticizing your partner's ideas. **Ask yourself if you want control in every situation or an intimate marriage.**

Remember that your man relies on your strength as his helper and homemaker. Without you, his cup is half-full, and God has made you to support, encourage, love, and help him lead his family.

**Today, as never before, God needs Spirit-filled wives who support their husbands' roles as family leaders.**

*"It is not good for the man to be alone. I will make a helper suitable for him."* Genesis 2:18.

**Meditate:** The inward joy of achievement that comes when your part is well done.

## REFLECTIONS

## CHAPTER 3

# Wisdom in the Family

*Some people are born into wonderful families,*
*Others have to find or create them.*
*Being a member of a family is a priceless membership*
*that we pay nothing for but love.*
Jim Stovall

The daily pressures of living as a family in the twenty-first century are incredible. You have often heard someone say, '*Oh, for the good old days.*' Let us not be fooled, for those who lived through the latter part of the twentieth century also had many challenges. Even the best or worst family situation teaches us about having a strong family bond.

I believe the difference today is that our lives move at a faster pace, and we are bombarded with meeting deadlines, technology, higher volumes of traffic, and higher living costs, just to name a few of the daily pressures a family must face. What we get because of this constant pressure on our family, is, too often, depression, stress, loss of happiness, worry, anxiety and even suicide.

Right now, are you one of the many who feel fatigued and would love to give up?

Don't give up, for we all feel the pressure of life at some point, and you must not abandon ship amid everything that makes up your family. No one has been entirely immune from pressure and stress, regardless of what century they lived in.

**Too often, we express our irritation and anxiety at those we love with the result of more strained relationships than any family can cope with.** Too many of us feel frustrated and hurt, and we release our pent-up emotions at each other; as a result, our children are often unfairly disciplined and learn to fear confrontation, which can lead to anxiety.

What we so often overlook is what God's Word has to say about wisdom for living in harmony as a family. In Ephesians 5:31-6:4, we read, *"For this reason a man will leave his father and mother and be united to his wife, and the two will become one flesh…*

*Each one of you also must love his wife as he loves himself, and the wife must respect her husband.*

*Children, obey your parents in the Lord, for this is right. "Honor your father and mother"—which is the first commandment with a promise...*

*Fathers, do not exasperate your children; instead, bring them up in the training and instruction of the Lord."*

Just as God wants His body (the church) to live together in harmony, He longs for the same harmony within our family life.

Sometimes, knowing how to hang out together as a family can be difficult. As parents, you may decide to pass on your values to your children. If you enjoy nature, having fun playing together, or sports of any type, your children will most likely also enjoy and value these.

Even though it may not always be picture perfect, remember that each activity you do together teaches them new skills and behaviour. Look for creative ideas to build an atmosphere where each family member is delighted to participate in, and responsible for helping create a family life of peace, contentment, and happiness.

Parents, you are the ones responsible for your children. Firstly, if there are any problems in your family life, like stress, tension or pressure, you need to determine the cause and how these issues within the family can be avoided. In doing this, you will need to consider –

- Changing some of the priorities of your family life.
- Is there someone in the family who could lessen the pressure if their **attitude changed?**
- Could **better planning** help minimise the tensions? – **WORK SMARTER, NOT HARDER.**
- Consider if there are too many commitments to outside clubs, meetings and other events.
- As a family, do you need to get more sleep and have a better diet?
- Are you taking time off to relax as a family?
- Is either parent spending too much time away from the family to be with friends?
- Are you trying to do too much?

## Responsibility

As parents, we are to set the example of harmony, living together in love and striving to create an atmosphere of peace within our homes. **Our children will live out what they learn from us. We are like God's letter to them;** they read us daily, even when they are very young.

We must be willing to work together and love our children, showing commitment and selflessness to create a family life for those in our care. **The most important part either parent can play in the family is praying for their spouse and children every day**. Naturally, this is more empowering for your family when you can communicate and pray together.

Both parents and children must do their part to bring harmony to the family environment. Some of the God-given responsibilities of every family member are to be thoughtful, considerate, and cheerful. When we speak kindly and truthfully to each other, pray, or work together, everyone will enjoy peace and harmony within the family unit.

## Attitude

**Attitude is our outward expression or opinion about something or someone, shaped by our feelings or thoughts.**

Attitude affects everything and everyone within our family. Our outward expression on our face or the words we speak shows what we think or feel within, whether good or bad. **It is essential that both parents have a positive attitude toward each other and their children.** It is a wise saying we find in Proverbs 17:22, *"A joyful heart is good medicine, but a broken spirit dries up the bones."*

Attitude is contagious. We have all experienced what happens to a family when one person reveals a negative attitude, or how the whole atmosphere is lifted when one expresses love and acceptance.

Paul described this in Romans 7:19, *"For I have the desire to do what is good, but I cannot carry it out. For I do not do the good I want to do, but the evil I do not want to do—this I keep on doing."* Maintaining a positive attitude can only be achieved by having an obedient attitude to our spiritual growth. James Allen said, **'A person cannot travel within and stand still without.'** When our attitude is conducive to positive growth, our mind expands, and attitude change happens.

John Maxwell once said, *'Do you feel the world is treating you well? You will receive excellent results if your attitude toward the world is excellent. If you feel so-so about the world, your response to that world will be average.* **Feel bad about your world, and you will seem to have only negative feedback from life.'**

In a family, our attitude is essential to the well-being of every member, whether small or adult children. We often find ourselves waiting for the other person to change rather than acknowledging that they are responsible for their own behaviour. The good news is that through prayer, God can change any one of us and teach us to have a natural positive outlook. **We create our environment by developing a positive** mental, emotional, physical and spiritual attitude regardless of circumstances.

## Our attitude to family life

- Don't let negative past experiences paralyse your attitude.

- We were designed to enjoy our work, remembering it is not what you do but how you do what you do that matters. Within the family, everyone benefits from a job that is well done. **LAZINESS comes naturally, but DILIGENCE has to be learnt.**

- Don't resent parents and partners because of the way they are. Keep yourself positive and move forward.

- Do everything with a positive attitude and don't seek praise from other family members.

- If you aren't good at something, get some training.

- **Routine family work is part of life. Accept it without complaining and enjoy the result.**

- A list (paper for personal; visual for family) that can be marked off gives a sense of completion and happiness.

- Do the most important things first and don't have too many projects simultaneously. **Finish one thing at a time** to receive a sense of achievement.

- Make time every day to spend together as a family. **Dinner without TV or phones can be a good time for each member to share something about their day.** If someone has had a bad experience, praying together for that person is good.

- Learn to laugh and see the humour in a situation. It is a marvellous way to release stress and pressure.

- Trust God to change the negative attitudes; remembering **change takes time, so be patient.**

- Dwell on the positive and thank God for everything (good or bad).

- **Most important** – Read God's Word and pray together as a family every day.

<u>Attitude Challenge</u> - **For a whole week without a single expectation, treat everyone in your family as the most important person in your life. You will find that they will start treating you in the same positive way.**

## The Challenges of family life.

Maintaining balance in a family of the twenty-first century is challenging as many demands are placed on each family member, especially on parents. As parents, it is necessary to maintain balance, which is often determined by the temperament of both.

If we look at the life of Jesus when He was on earth, despite all He had to do and all the challenges He faced, He maintained balance in his life by trusting God, and in doing so, He didn't allow pressure to overtake Him.

**Finding balance can make a big difference to living with stress.** Every family has demands like communication, availability, listening and daily chores. Every person within a family needs to grow physically, intellectually, socially and spiritually, as each of these is important to the health and well-being of each family member. In Luke 2:52, we read, *"And Jesus grew in wisdom and stature, and in favour with God and man."* To achieve this balance, we need to be organized in our homes, do everything correctly and in order, be flexible and **avoid being over-fastidious and inflexible**.

Being organized means finding simplicity and joy in everything you do. In other words, it means working smarter and not harder.

- **Establish a purpose** around which everything fits –

  1. Maintain your relationship with God.

  2. Have respect and discipline within the family.

  3. Encourage each member of your family in love and acceptance.

  4. Help each other develop their God-given gifts.

- **Establish Goals.** As parents, setting spiritual and material goals for your family is healthy. Goals need to be written down for future reference. Things like praying together as a family, attending church every week, and having your own home. I encourage you to write down your short-term and long-term goals, prioritise them and don't have too many.

- Make time each week to **relax together.** Sports events or even a swim together can be relaxing times.

- Live one thing, one day at a time. **Don't run your day by worrying about all you have to do.** (I have often heard someone say, '*I have so much to do.*') Be disciplined, and don't drive yourself. **WORK SMARTER, NOT HARDER.**

- Make time to spend with relatives and friends.

- **BE ORGANIZED**—Being organized will help you find simplicity in what you do, bring you joy, and give you more free time to do what is essential for a family. The following proven principles ("HANDY HINTS") will help your home be a place of freedom and peace but always presentable.

- **DON'T MAJOR ON THE MINORS.** Prioritize what matters most because the rest distracts from the important things.

When you have balance, you will find peace of mind, emotional strength, and inner confidence that God is guiding you as parents to meet life's challenges. *"Better one handful with tranquillity than two handfuls with toil and chasing after the wind."* (Ecclesiastes 4:6)

## HANDY HINTS:

- Accept family life as part of God's will for you and choose to do it well.

- **Learn to organize your home, or it will organize you**. *"But everything should be done in a fitting and orderly way."* (1 Corinthians 14:40). Organize one thing at a time and keep it in order.

- Have a place for everything–**DON'T JUST PUT IT DOWN, PUT IT AWAY**.

    a. Don't drop anything at the front door.

b. As you cook, put things away and tidy up as you work. **Clean as you go, there's always someone coming behind you.**

c. When you remove clothes, put them away or in the dirty basket. Remember, your children will learn from what they see you do.

d. Become someone who picks up and teaches your family to do likewise. Each child needs to understand that they must pick up their toys before bed. (This will need parents' help when young)

- Leave the kitchen clean, organized and tidy before bed at night.

- Go to bed at a sensible time to allow enough rest and sleep before your day starts

- Dress when you get up, and you will be amazed at what you achieve before work and school.

- Share the household jobs by having a board displaying the weekly work allocations. As your family grows, each should understand they have a part to play.

- Eat your meals together at the table (when possible). Saying grace or a prayer is excellent for starting the day. Clean up and leave the kitchen tidy after each meal.

- Have each family member hang up towels and pick up their clothes after using the bathroom.

- Sort laundry and have the first load in the machine ready to turn on when you get out of bed. Try not to have to wash every day.

- **Wash clothes when soiled**, not automatically after each time they are worn. Excess washing only increases your workload and decreases the durability of the clothes. Fold and put clothes away the day they are washed.

- Use good, easy, and nutritious recipes. Plan ahead and make a list so you only buy what is needed and don't overspend. Don't go to the store for just a couple of items unless absolutely necessary.
  Try new recipes to give variety and make you a creative cook. Cook extra and freeze for additional dinners or lunches. **Limit takeaway meals.**

- Encourage your children to have friends over for social times or meals.

- **CONSIDER HOW MUCH TIME IS SPENT ON SCREEN TIME.** Parents and families are time-poor because screen time frequently takes priority over daily tasks.

*"The purpose of life is not to be happy,
It is to be useful, to be honourable, to be compassionate,
to have it make some difference that
you have lived and lived well."*
Ralph Waldo Emerson

In Romans 12:10, Paul writes to the church in Rome, *"Be devoted to one another in brotherly love. Honour one another above yourselves."* If God wants this for His family (the church), how much more is it applicable to your family and mine?

We are to be committed to loving and caring for each other, being joyful and always hoping, patient when trouble strikes, and faithful in prayer. These are God-given practical ways to see the relationship within your family change as each member cares more for the others than themselves. The blessings your family will receive when you put Christ first will always exceed the cost to you, even when times are tough and hard to contend with.

If we want to transform chaos into order and foster peace, happiness, compassion, and laughter, **we need to place our Lord Jesus at the centre of our home**. Everything else should be approached with thoughtful consideration and care.

**Make a list of the things that are important for you to change and put them into practice as a family.** No family member is exempt from pressure and tension, so may I suggest you review these principles regularly to stop your family from slipping back into bad habits. If you, as parents, want to turn your home into a place where everyone finds comfort and happiness, you need to go back to the basic principles that have been proven to work throughout the centuries. Exchange your mask for honesty and cultivate a deep respect for the feelings of every family member.

## Living as an extended family

Family life in the twenty-first century has changed for many. Although living together has been shared and often expected in many cultures for multiple generations, this style of living has only existed in many countries since the late twentieth century.

Today, many families choose to live in extended family units to help children save for their own homes or provide a supportive environment for adult children looking for work or studying. This is also true when elderly parents are cared for by younger family members. Then there are also instances where a group of young adults choose to live together, not just to save on rent but to strengthen their bond and assist each other.

In each of these cases, where different generations with different ideas and values live together, there can be increased tension and conflict as each brings their ideas and expectations to the extended family relationship.

Just as when a husband and wife begin life together, each must value the other's strengths and work to make their relationship happy and respectful. The same applies to the extended family.

Upholding core values such as love and respect, loyalty, and communication are vital for an extended family living together to work successfully. These values are not just guidelines; they actively shape our decision-making, foster relationship-building, and enhance problem-solving skills. **Love and respect are particularly vital in fostering understanding and forgiveness**, which are essential in an extended family setup.

When embraced, these universal principles can bring unity and harmony to extended family living. They are applicable not just within a family but also in communities, nations, and our world. Let's consider these values and their role in fostering family unity and harmony.

**Complex relationships, conflicting loyalties and generational conflict** are some of the risk factors when entering an extended family relationship. While these challenges are real, they can be managed with the right approach and understanding, ensuring a harmonious extended family living experience.

## Love and respect

In Ephesians 6:2-3, Paul writes, *"Honour your father and mother"—which is the first commandment with a promise*

- *"so that it may go well with you and that you may enjoy long life on the earth."* While adult children are commanded to love and respect their seniors, there must also be respect for adult children from the seniors, especially when there is a separate family unit within the extended family.

Respect is demonstrated through our love and consideration for each other. In Romans 12:10, Paul says, *"Love each other with genuine affection, and take delight in honouring each other."* This verse encourages us to show genuine affection and how important each is to the other.

Senior parents should refrain from interfering in the discipline put in place by younger parents and instead adopt these principles out of respect for the parent's authority. They are invaluable in helping younger parents with small children by giving wisdom and guidance to the parents of the small children when it is sought. However, young parents must maintain discipline in their children, remembering that their parents have willingly opened their home and deserve respect from small children.

Senior parents must also love and respect the younger family to enable them to grow and develop as a separate family unit. They must be careful to respect the husband's rightful place within the younger family. This respect is essential as it can be difficult for young couples to build relationships within the extended family.

When a family shares love and respect for each other, encouragement and understanding naturally arise, especially during challenging times for one or more members. This adds unity and healthy feelings for each other.

## Loyalty

Loyalty within a family is the mutual shared obligations, responsibilities, and commitment to each other, forming a closeness or bond between family members. In Galatians 6:2, Paul says, *"Carry each other's burdens, and in this way, you will fulfill the law of Christ."*

Within the family, **loyalty means considering others before oneself and supporting others in good times and bad**. It's about **being honest, trustworthy, and generous**. To achieve this, healthy boundaries must be established that each family member agrees with.

The younger family should express gratitude to the senior parents for opening their home by contributing to household expenses and not expecting them to handle all the cooking and cleaning.

Loyalty is evidenced in things like being honest, showing care, apologizing when you are wrong, being willing to lose, and always showing others respect in what you say.

## Communication

Open and honest communication within the extended family is vitally important because it enables each member to discuss their needs, wants, and concerns in an atmosphere where they can express their differences or admiration for one another.

Before an extended family comes to live together, agreed-upon rules should be implemented, as not everyone shares the same lifestyle or way they live. The most important thing in setting these core rules is to **listen to each other's values and differences** so that each is considered and agreed upon. Considerations should include paying rent and utilities, maintaining cleanliness, being responsible, and managing pets.

Each family should establish clear boundaries that all members must honour. Important considerations include child discipline, curfews, mutual respect during partner disagreements, and how to handle household matters. (chores, cleaning, cooking, eating together, shopping, yard work, etc.).

Many families agree that the responsibility of doing chores is divided among the adults. Young adults need to be aware of regressing to their teenage lifestyle, leaving everything to their senior parents.

When families unite to save for a home, it's important to establish clear goals regarding the timeframe for saving. Senior parents should respect their children's readiness to leave and support their decisions when the time comes.

**Tips for successful Extended Family living.**

- Express your gratitude
- Give back, be responsible and grateful.
- Parents must respect the younger couples' autonomy and decision-making, only giving advice when requested.
- Resolve conflicts with understanding and agreement. Stay calm and put emotions aside. Listen without interrupting each person.
- Don't major on minors. Sometimes, this will call for sacrifice or turning the other cheek.
- Ask for help when needed.
- Communicate and talk together regularly

Extended family living calls for us to live in harmony and treat each member with respect, love and kindness. In Romans 12:16, Paul writes, *"Live in harmony with one another. Do not be haughty but associate with the lowly. Never be wise in your own sight."*

**"Humour is a great thing, a saving thing.** The minute it crops up, all our irritation and resentments slip away and a sunny spirit takes their place." (Mark Twain)

Laughing at your problems and life in general is beneficial to everyone. Some of us take things too seriously, even though we need to be serious at times and also have times to treasure. If we can laugh in the face of adversity, we will always enjoy life. **Life without laughter is not worth living.**

**Meditate:** God's generous treatment toward you commits you to generous treatment of others.

# REFLECTIONS

# CHAPTER 4

# Wisdom in Parenting

There are no fixed rules for parenting other than the principles God has laid out in His Word. In this chapter, I aim to help you understand what God says about parenting, alongside tried-and-true ideas that have worked for many families over many generations. Drawing from over fifty years of observing the dynamics between parents and their children and reflecting on the knowledge of the mistakes my husband and I made in our own family; I hope to share insights that can guide you on this journey.

As we watch our children navigate the world, a mix of apprehension and hope fills our hearts. We pray that they will grow into strong, resilient adults. Becoming a parent is much like planting a seed in a vast, empty field. In this journey, we are the farmers, tasked with nurturing our children through love, care, and guidance until they blossom into mature individuals—the true harvest of our efforts. Raising a child is a miraculous process, a beautiful beginning that unfolds over time, filled with potential and promise.

**Every child deserves to be loved, cherished, seen, known, and treasured by their parents. As parents, it's essential to nurture love rather than fear in your children; this foundation is crucial for their growth.** God has entrusted you with His precious gift to guide them safely as they navigate the perilous path to adulthood. Your role is to support them as they learn to cross the danger-filled street of life, helping them develop the confidence and resilience they need to thrive.

Proverbs 22:6 beautifully articulates our responsibility as parents: *"Start children off on the way they should go, and even when they are old, they will not turn from it."* **It's vital for children to feel unconditionally loved, and part of that love involves discipline and guidance.** Sometimes referred to as tough love, this approach is essential in helping our children grow into mature and responsible adults. By providing both affection and structure, we equip them with the tools they need to navigate life confidently.

Every child needs boundaries, and as parents, it's important to strike a balance between protection and independence. Just as we learned from our mistakes, so too will our children. **Remember, there is no such thing as a perfect child, and**

**striving for that ideal can be unfair to them.** Instead, allow them the freedom to be children, exploring and discovering their paths within the boundaries you set for them.

Unfortunately, many parents overlook the critical importance of their role. For countless children, lives are crushed by issues such as alcohol, abuse, incest, and other forms of maltreatment, leading to high rates of teenage suicide.

Socrates said, *"Fellow citizens, why do you turn and scrape every stone to gather wealth and take so little care of your children to whom one day you must relinquish it all?"* This serves as a powerful reminder that our children deserve our unwavering attention and love above all else.

Right back in Genesis, when the Lord appeared to Abraham and Sarah, we gain insight into the importance and responsibility of being parents. We read, *"For I have chosen him, so that he will direct his children and his household after him to keep the way of the Lord by doing what is right and just, so that the Lord will bring about for Abraham what he has promised him"* (Gen.18:19). This passage reminds us that guiding our children in faith and righteousness is not just a duty, but a vital part of fulfilling God's promises in our lives.

God placed importance on raising our children because He loves them and wants us as parents to **understand our responsibility to both Him and them.** Every child in every generation has a right to reach their human potential, yet too many struggle to meet the expectations that come with it. Instead of focusing solely on your expectations for your child, reflect on your ability to nurture and guide the fragile treasure you hold in your hands. **Rather than asking yourself what you expect from your child, ask yourself what you expect from your ability to guide God's gift to you.**

Just as we have a loving relationship with Jesus our Saviour, when we are God's children, we need to develop a heart-to-heart connection with our children. Without this bond, fear can take root, causing the child to feel apprehensive around you. As a parent, you are your child's primary mentor, and **the life you lead should reflect the values and qualities you wish them to mirror.**

In the twenty-first century, the expectations we place on our children often lead to an internal struggle that robs them of their childhood. We push them to act like adults before they have even had the chance to fully experience what it means to be a child. This pressure can create a war in their hearts, leaving them overwhelmed and unsure of themselves.

Children today face overwhelming pressure from excessive media exposure. By the time they turn sixteen, the average child will have spent over 18,000 hours in front of a screen and less than 15,000 hours in school, and every day, this gap continues to grow. Many parents are unaware that their children are exposed to explicit content, violence, and harsh realities in what they watch, and then we become shocked and despair when they engage in risky behaviour and crime as teenagers. It's essential to remember that **children learn not only from what we say but also from what we do and what they observe in our own media intake.**

Recently, I discovered that some parents today are coached on how to connect with their own toddlers and young children—something that should come naturally as a God-given instinct. When we observe the animal kingdom, we see that every creature has an innate drive to nurture their offspring to maturity, yet we, as humans, often struggle in this area. Parents, I encourage you to be actively engaged in the love and care of your child. **When you find yourself uncertain about what to say, take a moment to listen to what they are expressing. This simple act of listening can deepen your connection and understanding.**

As you read about wisdom in parenting, you will gain understanding and knowledge to enable you to have a close and trusting relationship with your children throughout life. A relationship where both you and your child can live without fear of anxiety and depression, being able to trust and enjoy life together. There is nothing quite like having the love and respect of your middle-aged children and young adult grandchildren when you reach a mature age.

Children today are maturing faster than ever, and many are grappling with questions about their gender identity. Parents, it's crucial to be aware of what your children are being taught, what they read, and what they watch online. These important conversations should be approached with love and openness, creating **a safe space where children feel free to ask questions without fear.** By guiding them through these complexities, you help them navigate their journey with confidence and understanding.

A large percentage of teenagers are already engaged in having sex and a number of these often without consent. They are also usually the victims of unreported rape or incest. It is reported that girls of 10 or 11 years often fear that if they are too friendly with another girl, there may be something wrong with themselves or how they are perceived. Although it should be perfectly natural for them to have close friends without modern society labelling them.

Our precious children today often experience immense pressure and are forced to make decisions that should be reserved for adults. This is especially true when the family unit breaks down, leading to a lack of structure in their daily lives. In such environments, children often feel lost and overwhelmed, highlighting the need for stability and support as they navigate their formative years.

Structure in a child's life is essential for their growth and social development. In some families where abuse is the norm, children may react by lashing out at their parents, a cycle that can extend into adulthood and lead to abusive marriages or other relationships. Other children, facing similar challenges, may retreat into a fantasy world, isolating themselves from society. This withdrawal can have long-lasting effects, often resulting in mental health issues in adulthood. I encourage you to **provide a nurturing environment where children feel safe and supported,** helping them break free from these harmful patterns.

As parents, you only have 15-18 years to prepare your children for life in our world of challenges. In the grand scheme of their lives, this is a brief window to instil in them the skills they need to thrive—spiritually, financially, physically, emotionally, and mentally. While it's inevitable that we will make mistakes along the way, what truly matters is getting the big things right. **Your children will remember the love, understanding, discipline, and praise you provide, which will lay a strong foundation for their future.**

Many parents today genuinely strive to do the right thing, but the overwhelming number of ideas and opinions can lead to confusion, often resulting in outcomes that differ from their intentions. We need to discover what God has to say and connect with the loving instincts He has instilled in us. By grounding our parenting in His wisdom, we can provide the support and guidance our children truly need.

**We must dedicate time in prayer for our children,** seeking God's guidance as parents and asking Him to grant our children the understanding and wisdom they need to become the adults He intends them to be in this world. Today, many parents, instead of embracing their role in guiding their children, tend to overprotect their children, treating them with excessive delicacy. However, there are times when a little tough love is necessary for true growth and learning.

Too often, in good faith, we feel and think we are doing what is best, only to find that down the track, we have made a significant mistake. I pray you will find wisdom and knowledge to help you love and discipline your children as well as to show compassion to yourselves as parents.

I don't have all the answers, especially when it comes to children with special needs. These children often require professional support and specialized skills to thrive in as normal an environment as their parents can provide.

In the following pages, I have endeavoured to help you, as parents of children today, find some ideas and principles that will better enable you to raise your precious children to be responsible, God-fearing citizens.

In Psalm 127:5, we read, *"Children are a heritage from the LORD, offspring a reward from him."* **Our children are a gift from God, and as parents, we are responsible to our God to train them and pray over them daily.**

## Respect and Responsibility

When we think of respect, we must understand that **not only do our children need to learn to respect their parents and other adults, but as parents, we must also show them respect in return**. In Ephesians 4:31-33 Paul emphasises how important it is to *"Get rid of all bitterness, rage and anger, brawling and slander, along with every form of malice. Be kind and compassionate to one another, forgiving each other, just as in Christ God forgave you."* This mutual respect and kindness creates a foundation for healthy relationships within the family.

If you wish to gain your child's respect, you must start from an early age to be the loving, firm and strong leader they will look up to. **Maintain firmness and love within boundaries and avoid giving in just for the sake of peace**. Taking these early steps will help prevent the development of antisocial behaviour. Teaching respect to preschoolers can be challenging, but if you can persevere in helping them control their impulsive and strong desires, you will gradually see improvements that will benefit them in the long run. **Be aware to differentiate between a respectful and a fearful child.**

Our children learn from what we do as parents; as we respect each other and them, they, in turn, will respect us. If we have disbelieved or punished them unnecessarily, we must be prepared to admit our mistake and apologize. This demonstrates respect for them, and they will learn to apologize to their parents, siblings, or friends when they are wrong.

It is not unnatural for a child to question your values and even challenge you. When this happens, take the time to help them understand their behaviour and the concept of respect by engaging with them directly and calmly, maintaining eye contact. **Aim to mould their will rather than diminish it.**

As parents, it's essential to manage our anger in front of our children. **Never tell them that they are unwanted or that they are a mistake;** such statements can severely damage their trust and self-confidence, leading them to feel guilty whenever things go wrong.

Bill Graham, the great evangelist of the twentieth century, said, *"A child who does not respect their parents will have no respect for anyone."*

## *Tips to help develop respect and responsibility*

- **Celebrate Achievements:** Congratulate your child when they accomplish something and proudly display their certificates and photos of their successes.

- **Encouragement:** Encourage them to think and ask questions so that they receive their answers truthfully.

- **Create Personal Spaces:** Allow children to have private areas, like a cubby house, where they can feel a sense of ownership and responsibility.

- **Foster Creativity:** Provide materials available for creative expression, such as glue, pencils, paper, paints, and board games.

- **Model Love and Care:** Let your children witness the love and care you have for one another as parents, reinforcing a positive family dynamic.

- **Welcome Their Friends:** Always make their friends feel welcome in your home, promoting a sense of community.

- **Laugh and Play Together:** Spend quality time as a family through laughter and play, strengthening your bond as a family.

- **Be Sensitive to Feelings:** Never ridicule them. Instead, be sensitive to their feelings, which will help develop their self-confidence. Never embarrass any child in public.

- **Private Punishment:** If discipline is necessary, ensure it's carried out in private to maintain their dignity.

- **Offer Genuine Praise:** Be generous with compliments and praise, but **ensure it is genuine and deserved.** Never praise them for who they are because that is God's work. Acknowledge their efforts while emphasizing that God and you will always love them regardless of their mistakes.

- **Individual Attention:** Spend quality time with each child, loving them unconditionally to foster a strong connection.

- **Prioritize Health Needs:** Always attend to and prioritize their health needs to show that you genuinely care. **Neglect can cause them to lose respect as they grow up.**

- **Provide Enriching Resources:** Surround your children with good books and music. Engage them in positive projects and good children's and teenage programmes in the church and community that support their spiritual, emotional, mental, social, and physical development. **Encourage your teenage children to be connected to a strong spiritual youth group**.

- **Teach Healthy Attitudes:** As they grow, educate them about healthy relationships and God's teachings on intimacy, ensuring they have a solid understanding. They especially need to know God's teaching on sex.

- **Demonstrate a Strong Work Ethic:** Set an example of responsibility and tidy habits at home, helping them understand **the importance of having a good work ethic** as they begin their own jobs.

- **Encourage Independence:** Teach them self-reliance and the understanding that the world owes them nothing.

Involve them in household duties and personal habits from a young age to prepare them for the future.

- **Handle Disappointments:** Teach them how to cope with disappointments. This valuable lesson can begin at a young age by **teaching them that they can't have everything they want.**

- **Create Happy Memories:** Make your home a happy space where they are always welcome to express their feelings and ask questions.

- **Teach them Values:** Don't push them to be highly educated or driven by materialism.

- **Instil Respect:** Teach them the importance of respecting themselves and others while emphasizing that **privileges come with responsibilities.**

Rearing children is like holding a piece of wet clay in your hands: it requires a firm yet gentle grip. If you hold on too tightly, it may slip from your grasp, but a gentle touch allows you to mould them as they explore and test the boundaries set by loving parents. Undoubtedly, children bring life to a home, naturally mimicking their parents. They can find just as much joy in discovering a big green tree frog as they do in playing with the latest fancy toy.

## Training - Dare to Discipline

In Proverbs 3:11, we read, *'My son, do not despise the Lord's discipline and do not resent his rebuke, because the Lord disciplines those he loves, as a father the son he delights in.'* This verse reminds us that if we love our children, our Heavenly Father expects us to discipline them with the same care and intent.

**As a parent, it's essential to first discipline yourself.** You can't lead your child or expect certain behaviours from them if you're not modelling those behaviours in your own life. Remember, children mirror what they see in you and what you do. For instance, avoid yelling at them about the mess in their room if your own room, office, or garage is disorganized. Leading by example is key to fostering respect and responsibility.

**Teach them how to make their bed and keep their clothes picked up.** This might sound unnecessary, but if they don't learn how to do the little things, **they will have difficulty in mastering the big issues of life.** This is why our armed forces discipline and inspect beds every day.

When disciplining a child, it's crucial for you, as the parent, to maintain a calm spirit, even if you're feeling overwhelmed and screaming inside. This can be particularly challenging with a determined or strong-willed child. However, staying calm and patient is essential for achieving the desired outcome, as **your** ability to maintain control will significantly influence the outcome of the situation.

I have broken Discipline into three headings: **Obedience, Structure and Routine, and Boundaries.**

<u>Obedience:</u>

Most parents want obedience from their children, but too often, we find ourselves yelling orders, sending them to time out, or even resorting to physical punishment. **It is important to be cautious about becoming a control freak through constant yelling.**

Whilst these disciplines have their place in certain situations, **what really matters is connecting with your child on a heart-to-heart level.** When children feel free to approach you, knowing that even though they have made mistakes and consequences will follow, you still love and understand them, it fosters a deeper bond. If parents can maintain love during those critical moments of disobedience, they can preserve their child's respect and hopefully encourage obedience.

Remember, you live in a home, not a showcase; things will naturally get out of place and sometimes become messy. **Getting angry about every situation does not promote obedience.** However, setting aside time for tidying and cleaning together is essential, as this helps teach discipline and fosters a sense of shared responsibility.

As you discipline your children, remember that you are nurturing a relationship with them. **Make it a priority to communicate love and compassion while guiding them to make positive choices and act justly.** Aim to set aside feelings of anger and disappointment, focusing instead on teaching them with understanding and kindness.

**Remembering your own childhood can help you to understand your children better.** As parents, we often speak over our children, leaving them confused and unable to express themselves. It's essential to empathize with their perspective and communicate effectively rather than placing unrealistic expectations on them and resorting to yelling. **Every child has a right to be heard.**

If you find it necessary to implement a form of punishment due to bad behaviour—whether it's a gentle smack on the bottom (not harsh punishment, which is abusive), time-out, or withholding a privilege—take a moment to ensure that both you and your child are calm before addressing the issue. **Sit down together and explain why their behaviour was unacceptable.** It's essential never to threaten a child with discipline unless you are prepared to follow through immediately after the offence occurs. Failing to do so can create a sense of dishonesty, leading to a lack of trust in what you say.

Parents should carefully consider together, the form of punishment they choose to implement. Once a decision has been made, it's essential to stand by it and not reverse it. Also, never interfere when the other parent is addressing a situation or administering punishment. This consistency reinforces the importance of discipline and supports an agreed united front.

A child's behaviour comes from how they interpret the world around them. Are they witnessing freedom, love, respect, and self-control in their parents' lives? As parents, you must display these attributes daily, as they are powerful examples for your children.

God knew that every parent would face days when their children would try their patience, so He provided clear instructions about discipline. It is important to start this process from day one. Proverbs 22:6, we read, *"Start children off on the way they should go, and even when they are old, they will not turn from it,"* and then in Proverbs 29:15, *"A rod and a reprimand impart wisdom, but a child left undisciplined disgraces its* (parents) *mother."*

Today, in the twenty-first century, some parents think that these instructions are outdated. However, **if we disregard God's instructions, we risk inviting failure into our parenting.** God wants us to teach them that He loves them, and in turn, we must also love them. They must understand the difference between right and wrong and how their choices can impact their relationship with Him and you, as their parents. Ephesians 6:4 reminds us, *"Fathers,* (parents) *do not exasperate your children; instead, bring them up in the training and instruction of the Lord."*

***Parent's prayer***
*'Help us each day to realize the astounding responsibility that is ours.*
*O Lord, hold onto our children's hands and assist us to love, discipline, and guide them every day in Your ways.'*

## Structure and Routine

Today, families come in many shapes and sizes, and while we often think of the traditional structure of a father, a mother, and at least one child, this is just one of many ways to define family. For a long time, society has held the conventional nuclear family as the 'ideal' setting for raising children. However, the reality is that many families thrive outside this model. If you find yourself a single parent due to circumstances beyond your control, know that your family is just as valid and can be filled with love.

Regarding family structure, what truly matters, regardless of your circumstances, is your shared goal of raising healthy and happy children. This is achieved through the guidelines and values that parents put in place, helping each child learn discipline, respect, and responsibility.

In addition to these essential principles, various aspects bring structure to family life, which we, as parents, need to teach and model for our children. Through years of observing families, I've noticed that many parents act in good faith, believing they are doing what's best, often without considering the long-term impact of their choices. It's crucial that every family member feels happy and content while also learning to live together harmoniously as a united family.

In this portion, we will explore important aspects of everyday family living that can help your child grow into a responsible adult with the strength and stability needed to navigate the world beyond their family environment.

**Every child wants to feel needed and have a routine that is followed.** When they have something to offer to the running of the home, it gives them a sense of responsibility to their parents and siblings and is the beginning of training them to have a good work ethic.

Many families have a flow chart on the fridge or notice board, setting out the jobs allocated to each family member, including mum and dad. Naturally, as parents, there will be far more to do than what is listed, but having your names there helps your children feel valued and accountable.

From when a child can communicate and even before they are walking, encourage them to help you put their toys into the appropriate box. As they grow and start school, make a chart for the week where each day is ticked off for doing the required task. Keep their daily responsibilities manageable, allowing plenty of time for them to accomplish their tasks while still being able to enjoy playtime.

Every child should have some chores to do each day, like setting the breakfast or dinner table, putting their dirty clothes in the washing basket, putting toys away, keeping their rooms tidy, making their bed and feeding their pets. Encouraging these responsibilities fosters a positive attitude and can extend to many other tasks. As they grow and come to understand their chores, they can become more responsible, giving them a good work ethic, self-control, punctuality and self-worth, qualities that will serve them well when they enter the workforce.

**Lighten your load** by teaching your children essential skills like how to shower, clean their teeth and dress themselves by the time they start school, or sooner if possible. All these things will lighten your workload as parents while providing good life skills for your children.

This is also an excellent time to start teaching them how to use money wisely and that it comes from working. At the end of the week, they can receive pocket money, which they can divide into three amounts. One is for them to save for spending, one to save, and one to give away. Using three labelled containers can make this process fun and engaging. When they practice generosity, they'll experience the joy of kindness, learning that kind children are happy children. These principles will also teach them about setting goals, delayed gratification, and empathy.

Parents need to help their children understand the importance of persisting and focusing to achieve their goals in life. When they are young, these things can be taught just in the small chores they are given to do around the house, and then when they are in school, they can apply these principles to achieve their goals both academically and in their sporting activities. **Never tell your child that their goal is too high to achieve.** As parents, we must encourage them to strive for success; otherwise, we risk giving them an excuse to believe they cannot achieve their dreams and goals.

As parents, it's important to ensure that chores are completed and to offer help when needed. **Avoid being the parent who sits on the couch, browsing the web, and calling out,** 'Have you finished yet?' This behaviour signals a lack of interest in your child. When they become teenagers, you might find yourself frustrated by constantly telling them to get off their phones, yet **they are simply reflecting the example you've set.**

When a family functions as a team, they will learn that life is not just about them but also that their contribution brings worth and respect to their parents and siblings.

## Boundaries

**Boundaries are an excellent way to help a child of any age understand your expectations of them.** As parents, we also have boundaries in our own lives that hopefully reflect our love and respect for our God. When you have spent time showing love while being firm and strong in your guidance, they will understand what acceptable behaviour is through the boundaries you have established. If you have failed to set clear boundaries at an early age, it's important to recognize that you can't hold them accountable if they break your assumed boundaries. An excellent book on Boundaries is, 'Boundaries with Kids,' by Drs. Cloud and Townsend.

Proverbs 13:24, *"Whoever spares the rod hates their children, but the one who loves their children is careful to discipline them."*

Someone once said, *'Apply the rod of correction to the seat of learning from time to time.'*

## *Tips on discipline*

- **Begin at infancy, and don't give your child everything they want.** Every day, parents offer their children choices about what they eat, what they wear and countless other things in many other aspects of life. This can lead to **children believing that the world owes them something and that life revolves around fulfilling their desires.** As parents, we need to understand that a small child does not know what foods are nourishing or what clothes to wear; this is our responsibility.

- **Most importantly, tell your child frequently that you love them.** They need to hear **'I love you'** often. Show them affection by touching and hugging them, reinforcing their uniqueness. **When children feel accepted, they learn to love in return.** Use your eyes to convey pride and affirmation, showing them your acceptance and support.

- EVERY CHILD ALIVE MUST KNOW THAT **'NO' MEANS 'NO'** *"Simply let your 'Yes' be 'Yes,' and your 'No' be 'No; anything beyond this comes from the evil one."* (Matt.5:37). When we gently, firmly, and consistently say no to children, we teach them the importance of setting boundaries for themselves, equipping them to be able to say no to the things they will encounter in life that they know they should avoid.

- Support them with encouraging words so they feel free in their heart and lives. While you cannot give them freedom, you can create an environment that nurtures them. **Be careful not to push them away with negative thinking.**

- **Never be too busy to listen to them.** Don't frustrate them by ignoring them when you are watching TV or reading. While it may seem an inopportune time, remember they grow up very quickly. Make the effort to spend quality time with them, and you won't regret it.
**Will they listen to your discipline if you ignore them?**

- **Don't make empty threats – follow through on what you say.** Your child may ask, "Can we get ice cream?" You say, "No." The child will push and negotiate, and thinking you are solving the problem, you say, "Fine, we'll get ice cream today, but don't ask me tomorrow because the answer is no!" Your child has just won. Later, you wonder why they won't take 'no' for an answer. **Your child won't take 'no' for an answer because the answer is never no!**

- **Don't discipline by yelling.** Yelling can instil fear and angry outbursts, often leading to increased rebellion, which can escalate a parent's frustration. Speak to them softly and with respect. **When discipline is firm, clear and consistent, it provides a sense of security for the child.**

- Remain calm and be tolerant, as **your attitude affects the outcome of the situation**

- **Avoid laughing when they use inappropriate language or misbehave.** This can lead them to believe their actions are acceptable and encourage the development of bad language and habits

- **Avoid using the word WRONG too frequently,** as overuse can lead a child to continually feel guilty, which fosters the belief that society is against them later in life. **A child who lives in FEAR learns to be APPREHENSIVE**

- **Don't pick up everything they leave lying around.** From an early age, train them to understand how to put their own things away. Teach them to put their clothes and toys, etc., where they belong – Teach them – **"DON'T PUT IT DOWN, PUT IT AWAY".**

- **Be aware of what your child is reading and watching** to ensure their minds are not exposed to negative influences.

- **Don't argue in front of your children.** Parents who argue in front of their children often find that their children will grow up arguing with their parents, believing it is acceptable behaviour.

- From an early age, **guide your children's food choices instead of giving them free rein,** which can lead to poor eating habits. Allowing too much choice can foster a sense of entitlement, making them believe they can have whatever they wish. Teaching denial can be beneficial in preventing harmful frustrations.

- **Keep mealtimes happy, sitting at the table together with the TV off.** This creates a warm atmosphere where everyone can share their day and engage in meaningful conversations. It encourages connection and strengthens family bonds, helping children feel valued and heard. Establishing this routine can also promote healthy eating habits and a sense of togetherness.

- **Always approach situations with an open mind** and never take your child's side against their friends, neighbours, teachers, or the police without fully understanding the circumstances first. It's important not to assume that others are against your child, as conflicts often arise from a lack of guidance or discipline on your part. Take the time to gather all the facts so you can help support your child while teaching them the value of accountability and perspective.

- **Avoid criticizing anyone in front of your children.** This sets a poor example that can influence how they perceive and treat others. Instead, model respectful and constructive communication, demonstrating the importance of addressing others with kindness and understanding.

- **When your child faces consequences for their own mistakes, avoid apologizing on their behalf.** Help them understand the importance of taking responsibility for their actions. Refrain from saying things like, "I can't do anything with him/her," in front of others, as this undermines their accountability and may affect their self-esteem. Encourage open conversations about their behaviour, guiding them toward learning and growth.

- Show value to the chores they do so that they enjoy doing them, being generous with praise.

- Allow them to express their feelings and ask questions. **This is important when disciplining them.** This is essential for their understanding and emotional growth.

- **Assist your children in learning to make decisions, teaching them about making good and bad choices.** Do not be afraid of their mistakes, instead; recognize that poor choices are important in learning, as they need to have the opportunity to understand choosing between good and bad. By allowing them the freedom to choose, you help them understand the value of making informed decisions and empower them to differentiate between right and wrong.

- **Assist your children in navigating disappointment,** teaching them that they cannot always have everything they desire. Learning to cope with setbacks helps build resilience and a realistic understanding of life's limitations.

- Remember that children grow and learn by testing the boundaries set by their parents. **Help them understand that there are consequences when they act outside these boundaries.** This guidance keeps them safe and teaches them valuable lessons about responsibility and respect.

- **Avoid interfering with your partner's discipline.** Doing so can lead your child to test you against each other. It's crucial to remain calm and supportive when discipline is being administered, especially if your spouse is the one guiding the process. This united front reinforces consistency and helps your child understand the importance of respecting boundaries.

- Be aware that when you count down the time for them to do something, it gives your child time to consider their response. Children are often more perceptive than we realize. **Communicate your expectations clearly and follow through with the appropriate consequences without hesitation if necessary.**

- Spend time enriching what your children learn at school. For example, board games can be excellent tools for teaching concepts like money management, multiplication, and spelling. Engaging in these activities as a family strengthens your bond and allows you to share valuable insights about life and the world around them.

- To discourage lying, avoid punishing your child for actions they openly confess. However, it's essential to address any deliberate or rebellious behaviour, ensuring it doesn't go unnoticed. This will encourage honesty while still emphasizing the importance of accountability.

- Give them pocket money for their jobs, teaching them how to value money.

## Commitment and knowing God's blessing

When we bring children into this world, as parents, we must cultivate self-discipline. In Hebrews chapter 12, the writer speaks about God's discipline, *"My son, do not make light of the Lord's discipline, and do not lose heart when he rebukes you, because the Lord disciplines the one he loves, and he chastens everyone he accepts as his son. No discipline seems pleasant at the time but painful. Later on, however, it produces a harvest of righteousness and peace for those who have been trained by it."*

Make it a daily practice to provide your family with spiritual guidance. Begin with Bible stories and prayer, whether it's saying grace before meals or offering a short prayer each morning. As your children attend church and engage in the children's programs, you'll have wonderful opportunities to teach them deeper values that will last a lifetime.

When you reflect on everything you teach your children, it's easy to see how the precious moments spent praying and sharing God's love can get overshadowed by the demands of daily life. In the hustle and bustle, it's important to prioritize this foundational teaching, ensuring that their understanding of God's love remains at the forefront of their lives.

In the light of eternity, they need to know that they are loved by both God and you before anything else. Psalm 103:17, *"But from everlasting to everlasting the Lord's love is with those who fear him, and his righteousness with their children's children."*

**Remember, your children are on a learning journey.** They are naturally inclined to make mistakes, and as parents, we can sometimes become so fearful of their mistakes that **we unintentionally teach them to be afraid.** God doesn't control our lives as parents, and we shouldn't try to intimidate our children with excessive control. Instead, let's embrace the truth that we, including our children, have been given a spirit of power, love, and self-control (2 Timothy 1:7).

A vital part of their learning journey is developing self-control through the respect, understanding, discipline, obedience, and love we, as parents, impart to them. Our behaviour and self-control are not just for our children's sake; we are ultimately answerable to our Heavenly Father for how we guide them.

Small children often get fearful at night and can't sleep. Teach them little prayers that they can say for themselves.

> *'God of heaven, see me now,*
> *Beneath the stars, the moon and clouds.*
> *Grant me dreams to sleep in peace,*
> *And with the sunrise in the east,*
> *Wake me to a glorious day,*
> *Dear Lord Jesus, I pray.'*

- **Create Happy Memories:** Build joyful experiences into the life of your child.

- **Family Outings:** Have special outings with just parents and children to strengthen your bond.

- **Be a Role Model:** Set a positive example through your words and actions. Children learn to navigate boundaries by observing how their parents respond to the limits set by the world.

- **Listen Actively:** Children learn to navigate boundaries by observing how their parents respond to the limits set by the world.

- **Consistent Discipline:** Commit to how you want to discipline with a clear approach and stick to it. Always remember to avoid criticizing them in front of others.

- **Apologize When Necessary:** It can be challenging to say sorry, but acknowledging your mistakes shows your child that perfection is not the goal.

- **Practice Calmness:** Children dislike anger and being yelled at. They thrive when they feel understood, so approach discipline with patience. **Yelling can instil fear and may lead them to distance themselves from your values.**

- **Avoid Favouritism:** Treat each child equally, as favouritism can lead to resentment and hurt between siblings.

- **Understand Their Choices:** As children grow, they may make choices that can hurt you, such as getting involved in substance abuse or crime. Remember that each child is responsible for their own decisions. Though it can be heartbreaking, always respond with love and patience, allowing them the opportunity to seek forgiveness.

- **Reflect on Your Child's Environment:** Ask yourselves if your children are living with:

    **CRITICISM** – which teaches them to condemn.

    **HOSTILITY** – which encourages them to fight.

    **FEAR** – which makes them apprehensive.

    **PITY** – which leads them to feel sorry for themselves.

    **RIDICULE** – which fosters shyness.

    **JEALOUSY** – which instils guilt.

- **Or are they experiencing:**

    **TOLERANCE** – which helps them learn patience.

    **ENCOURAGEMENT** – which builds their confidence.

    **PRAISE** – which fosters appreciation.

**ACCEPTANCE** – which teaches love.

**APPROVAL** – which helps them like themselves.

**RECOGNITION** – which inspires them to set goals.

**HONESTY** – which instils truthfulness.

**FAIRNESS** – which teaches them about justice.

**SECURITY** – which nurtures faith in themselves.

**FRIENDLINESS** – which shows that the world can be a nice place.

- **Stand Firm in Discipline:** Sometimes, as parents, we need to uphold our boundaries and have the courage to say no even when it's difficult.

- **Overindulgence:** Continuously giving, especially in terms of money, won't necessarily help them make better choices. Overindulging children with material things like toys, does not help them appreciate what they have.

I would encourage you, above everything else, to pray without ceasing for your children that God will work in their lives to make them the adults He wants them to be. Turn Ephesians 3:14-19 into a prayer, especially for each one and pray it over them every day.

Parenting can be both challenging and thankless, but it can also be one of the most important and rewarding tasks God has entrusted to us. Through prayer and the guidance of our Heavenly Father, we can make it a joyful and incredible privilege, dedicating ourselves to training our children to love God and others. For those parents who have embraced this blessing, we can only express our gratitude to God for His support and wisdom in fulfilling this responsibility.

Never be fooled into believing that if your child is doing what you say, then everything is fine. As soon as they are out of your presence, they are no longer under your control, and this is where the value of having taught them the benefit of self-control comes into play. They will very often realize their own mistakes and return to the core values they know.

When you have built a heart-to-heart connection, their decisions will depend on their relationship with you, their parent.

As parents, we have relied on fear-based punishment for too long. When we stop living in fear and anxiety and deeply connect with God, our relationships with our children can transform into what God desires for a happy family because there is no fear in love.

> *"Be shepherds of God's flock that is under your care, watching over them— not because you must, but because you are willing, as God wants you to be; not pursuing dishonest gain, but eager to serve; not lording it over those entrusted to you, but being examples to the flock. And*

*when the Chief Shepherd appears, you will receive the crown of glory that will never fade away."* (1 Peter 5:2-4)

## Anxiety

Although I have previously noted that children with some conditions and disorders require professional help, the condition of anxiety is one that I would like to make note of.

Most professionals tell us that children are not born with anxiety, although there are those with personalities and natures who have tendencies toward developing anxiety. Today, many primary school-age children have developed anxiety that requires professional help.

A frequently asked question by a counsellor or psychologist is what the patient remembers about their childhood. In most cases, the answer is relative to what they remember about their parents' behaviour, whether it be quarrelling, abuse, or being screamed or yelled at. Parents, **these issues can play a significant role in the development of anxiety in your child,** especially if they are of a sensitive nature. Unfortunately, these issues are often carried from one generation to the next.

To help overcome this problem within your family, may I suggest that if you as a parent suffer from these or any other issues, you seek professional help so that your children experience a positive and loving atmosphere in which to grow.

Also, seek spiritual guidance to grow your relationship with Jesus, your Saviour and friend. *"Fathers,* [parents] *do not embitter your children, or they will become discouraged."* Col.3:21.

Parents, be aware of refraining from anger and any other attitudes that can embitter their children and cause them anxiety.

## Strong-willed children.

Strong-willed children can be very frustrating and often push parents to their limits. In these moments, parents may feel the urge to break their child's strong will and resort to intimidation, forgetting that God's design is rooted in love with boundaries (Ephesians 3:15). It's essential to remember that **God has given your child a strong will and character for a purpose.**

When disciplining a strong-willed child, parents must remain calm and patient to achieve the desired outcome for the child.

As parents, we should strive to cultivate a relationship with our children that mirrors God's relationship with us. He blesses us for our obedience and provides consequences for our disobedience.

Having a strong-willed child is not a negative trait; it simply is part of who they are. Remember, this temperament is a gift from God for a purpose.

## *Some tips for training a strong-willed child.*

- **Choose Punishments Wisely:** Make sure your decisions are fair and well-considered, as a strong-willed child will remember them, and you can't go back on your choices.

- **Smacking:** While it may temporarily get your child's attention, smacking can quickly damage your connection with your strong-willed child, so try to avoid it. Prioritize their needs, not their wants.

- **Always Remain Calm and Tolerant:** Always maintain your composure when disciplining a strong-willed child.

- **Be aware of Your Stress Levels:** It's easy to lose control when stressed, which can lead to harmful reactions.

- **Follow Through on Consequences:** Without fail, always carry out the punishments you have communicated.

- **Avoid Threats:** Instead of using threats to get obedience, make sure that your life manifests the values you expect of them. They are more likely to obey when they see you living those principles.

- **Understand Their Testing:** Strong-willed children often test boundaries to gauge your determination. These children admire strength and courage, so demonstrate these qualities with love and patience. **They want to see you as their superhero.**

- **Gentle Communication:** Harshness, gruffness, and constant orders one after the other will have little effect.

- **Empathize with Their Perspective:** Consider how your discipline feels from their point of view and if you would respond positively to such discipline. This is the time to respect their feelings and discuss why their behaviour is unacceptable in a calm, face-to-face conversation.

- **Recognize Their Challenges:** A strong-willed child will challenge your authority. While their boldness may be amusing, please don't show it; otherwise, they might take advantage.

- **Patience is Key:** It can be frustrating as they test your patience to see if you are worthy of their respect.

- **Set Clear Boundaries.** Strong-willed children thrive with definite boundaries, even if they won't admit it. They often seek control, much like an untrained Terrier dog.

- **Sibling Dynamics:** They often clash with their siblings and feel misunderstood. For Example, a compliant child might appear innocent but can be sneaky, unlike a strong-willed child who is more overtly challenging. Be alert to all behaviours.

- **Avoid Power Struggles:** They often engage in power games and can be wilfully defiant. **Remember, every child is a blessing from God to you and your family.**

- **Conquer the Will, Not the Spirit:** It's essential to guide their strong will without breaking their spirit, which defines who they are.

- **Pray for Them:** Lay hands on them and pray for them, especially when they're asleep.

- **Treat All Children Equally:** Favouritism can create resentment; each child should feel valued.

- **Practice Empathy:** Try to see every situation through their eyes. God chose you as their parent because He knew that with His help, you would be able to discipline and guide them.

- **Consider an 'Affirmation Station':** Consider having a daily affirmation practice where your child chooses a card with positive statements like, 'I am thoughtful,' 'I am respectful,' and 'I am a good listener.'

## Your God-given opportunity

What an excellent opportunity God gives you as a parent when He places a little life into your hands and allows you to assist Him in moulding that little life into the person He intends them to become.

He allows you to be responsible for everything in your child's life. **So, how are you doing?**

As I have mentioned, I don't have all the answers; none of us do. **Only God has the wisdom to give us the answers we seek.** My prayer is that as you reflect on these thoughts about parenting, the Lord will reveal ideas that will help you achieve your goals for your children. We all act in good faith, striving to nurture each child according to their unique needs.

If you take nothing else from my words, please remember to love and support your children with positivity, nurturing them as they grow to have a heart for the Lord. Allow them to be free in their hearts as they grow so they will love and respect you in return. Most importantly, pray for your children every day, and if you are struggling in any area or with any one of them, take your concerns to the Lord and let Him work in their lives to shape them into who He wants them to be.

Children are very special to Jesus. In Matthew 19:14, He told the disciples, *"Let the little children come to me, and do not hinder them, for the kingdom of heaven belongs to such as these."*

And in Mark 10:16, we read how he blessed them. *"And he took the children in his arms, placed his hands on them and blessed them."*

I encourage you as parents to keep close to Jesus and experience how much He loves and cares for you. Learn from Him. He loved us when we were unlovely and then gave His life for us. **Love your children like that.** (Ephesians 5:1-2)

Your children will only know Jesus as they see your commitment to Christ mirrored in your life and how important it is for your family to **spend time every week worshipping God together in church. This needs to be your number one priority** and should always be above time spent socializing or going to sports events. Otherwise, they will not value their relationship with God.

*"He will love you and bless you and increase your numbers. He will bless the fruit of your womb, the crops of your land— in the land he swore to your ancestors to give you.* (Deuteronomy 7:13) And finally.

### ***Bring them to church.***
*Bring them to church. Saturate their*
*lives with the Word of God.*
*Even if they lie on the floor, even if they fall asleep.*
*Even if they need 200 'go-fish' cards and a sucker to be quiet.*
*Even if you stand in the back, swaying*
*back and forth, holding them.*
*Even when it's hard.*
*Even when your row looks like a small*
*hurricane just came through.*
*Bring them to church.*
*Let them see you worship. Let them see you pray.*
*Let them see you running toward the Saviour…*
*because if they don't see and learn these things from you,*
*who are they going to learn them from?*

*The world will teach them it's not a priority.
The world will teach them it's okay to lie
about and not pick up their Bibles.
The world will direct them so far off course, confuse them,
and misinform them that just being "good" is enough.
The world won't teach them about Jesus. That's our job.*
**Bring them to church.**

Attributed to Mother Teresa

# REFLECTIONS

# CHAPTER 5

# Wisdom with Finances

*Money is nothing more than a tool. It can be a force for good, a force for evil, or simply be idle.*
Jim Stovall

We recognize that an abundance of wealth can foster pride, tempting Christians to depend on their riches and distancing them from their relationship with God. On the other hand, poverty can create challenges in meeting our family's daily needs, sometimes leading individuals to resort to theft or take on undesirable jobs to provide for their loved ones. This underscores the delicate balance we must strive for in our financial lives—one that honours God and prioritizes our relationship with Him above our material circumstances.

Proverbs 30:7-9, *"Two things I ask of you, Lord; do not refuse me before I die: Keep falsehood and lies far from me; give me neither poverty nor riches, but give me only my daily bread.*

*Otherwise, I may have too much and disown you and say, 'Who is the Lord?' Or I may become poor and steal, and so dishonour the name of my God. A life is worth more than a bank account."*

When we acknowledge that God is the ultimate provider of our needs and place our complete trust in Him, He not only meets our needs but often exceeds them. If we can trust and find contentment in God's provision, we will always have more than enough.

Even when our budget feels tight, we shouldn't let worry about the future overwhelm us. God has instructed us to ask for our daily bread. As we diligently work and cooperate with God, we can trust that He will provide. He is the same God who miraculously fed the 5,000 in the past. Everything will fall into place when we envision our lives in our Heavenly Father's capable hands.

**Remember, where God is, there is always enough; the limitation lies within our lives to have faith to trust.** Our focus should be on God's kingdom, not on wealth. Ecclesiastes 5:10 reminds us, *"Whoever loves money never has enough; whoever loves wealth is never satisfied with their income."*

While we often credit our financial stability to our hard work, it's essential to remember that it is God who empowers us to work. He secures our positions and equips us for our daily tasks. Many of us can testify to His guidance throughout our lives in our various roles, where He has consistently met our needs. Even if we haven't been wealthy, we can confidently say, *"I have never lacked anything I needed and have always had more than enough."* This reflects God's faithfulness and His unwavering commitment to providing for us.

God expects us to provide for our families and not misuse our money on gambling, excessive alcohol or drugs, etc. *"Anyone who does not provide for their relatives, and especially for their own household, has denied the faith and is worse than an unbeliever"* (1 Tim.5:8).

In the business world, maintaining a certain amount of capital is also necessary to increase our business. When a man uses his money wisely, taking only what he requires as a legitimate profit, and then pays his employees a share of the extra, he is doing something more excellent than if he sold everything and distributed a small amount to a vast number of people.

God likes our participation because there is satisfaction and reward when we work and earn. What we worry about will limit our lives. **It is better to be wealthy on the inside and poor on the outside**. It's about living close to God.

God has blessed many with wealth so that we can use it to help others. Whatever we have, whether wealth or just enough, God wants us to be wise with our money. We need to appreciate and manage our money, as poor handling can cause a breakdown in our relationships. Often, the confusion caused by finances can be simply that no one has shown us how to discipline ourselves in the areas of spending and saving.

Overspending can lead to significant debt, which can create worry and sometimes make it difficult to secure a loan from the bank.

I have endeavoured to give you some simple, accurate, proven ideas that may help you, but I encourage you to seek professional help with your finances.

Let us learn together how to manage our finances with sacrifice and savings to be faithful stewards of God's provision.

## SAVE BEFORE YOU SPEND

This principle is most important, as it will be the means of your security. Some couples save 10% of their income and have a separate account for their savings. Most banks and financial institutions will transfer this amount each pay for you. **The important issue is deciding on an amount and not touching it.** Then, as it accumulates, seek advice about secure investment of your funds. Be wise, and only use this saved money in cases of emergencies like loss of income or severe illness.

- Outgoings must be less than your income.

- Live within your means.

## INSURANCE POLICIES

Insurance is an essential aspect of managing your income. Always ensure that any loans—especially your mortgage—are adequately covered. Keep in mind that today, insurance for your home or car is often included in your payments to the bank. Even in the unfortunate event of the primary income earner's death, a substantial investment can still be sold, allowing the family to transition to a smaller home and still provide them with some financial support.

Life insurance and income protection insurance are also essential. **Your ability to earn is your greatest asset.** Many couples wish they had listened to this advice when one parent has taken ill or passed away.

House and contents insurance, even though expensive, are essential. We have become more aware of this, as we see in the news media families losing their homes in storms, cyclones, and fires.

- Choose a higher excess which reduces your premium.
- Engage a good insurance agent who will search for the best value for your money or shop around for the best deals.

- Don't just automatically go with the same Company each year. Make sure they still have the best deal.

- Consider seriously whether you need private health insurance at this stage. It is expensive, and the gap fee can cost you a lot of money. If you earn over $100,000 annually, research the top cover policies before deciding.

# BUYING A HOUSE

Today, we often hear that the key to buying a home is "location, location, location." While this is undoubtedly important, it's also essential to consider the resale value, including factors like the number of bedrooms and available amenities. Before purchasing, speak with the bank to understand how much you can borrow and what your repayments will be. Additionally, always arrange for a pest and building inspection through a reputable builder to ensure your investment is sound.

- Make weekly payments instead of monthly payments, and you will be surprised at how much you can recoup from your loan over time.

- You need patience and persistence to realize your dream home; most likely, it will not always be your first home.

- Choose a home that is more than just a house, something that will bring your family happy memories.

- Think of ways to make your home more attractive without overspending.

If needed, seek sound wisdom from a trusted friend or your Solicitor.

## ADDITIONAL FINANCIAL ADVICE

### Credit Cards:

- Get into the habit of paying for everything if you can and avoid using Credit Cards as much as possible.

- If you have credit card debt, pay back your monthly spending. Otherwise, the interest on your debt will seriously affect your budget. If you only pay the monthly requirement on a $4,200 debt, it will take 42 years to pay back, and you will pay approximately $21,080 in interest. This amount could even be more significant depending on the interest rate.

- If you need to, cut them up so you can't use them.

- Avoid getting additional Credit Cards.

### Buying a Car:

- Buy a car you can afford, and if possible, pay cash or more than the minimum deposit.

- Don't change cars too often; you lose money quickly, especially on new vehicles.

- Instead of trading your vehicle, sell it privately.

**A sale is not always good:**

- A bargain is only a bargain if you need it, not if you are buying impulsively.

- Remember that everything drops in value after purchase, especially a car, furniture, clothes, and electrical goods.

- Try to buy quality, but only what your budget allows.

- Don't sacrifice your savings to obtain instant gratification

- Don't buy the first item, which may be the most expensive. Shop around.

- Don't waste money on too much fast food. You can wait 30 minutes for it, and it would only have taken you the same time to prepare a nourishing meal at home. Think of the money saved.

## BUDGET TO HAVE FREEDOM

Financial freedom can be achieved with discipline and planning. Don't be phased by Budgeting or Financial Planning; it is a simple process that can be achieved when you decide with your spouse where and how much of your money will be used for every family need. Make this exercise a positive step to financial freedom by setting goals and enjoying the rewards together.

Remember, God has called us to be good stewards of the money we earn through our ability to do the work He has given us. The first payment that should come from our wages is our gift of gratitude to our God. Proverbs 3:9 says, *"Honor the Lord with your wealth, with the first fruits of all your crops."* **God is the giver of every gift and will always honour generous people**.

It is best to have a good and safe plan to achieve freedom with the money you earn. **Those who fail to plan, plan to fail.**

It is time to sit down together and work out your plan, one that both are happy with and understand the part they must play in being honest with each other and working together to achieve your goal.

### Build your Freedom Plan.

- Firstly, sit down and decide on the percentage of your wages, after tax, that you will honour God's work with. You can autopay this to your Church account.

- Building your plan is about getting you out of debt and reaching financial freedom with long-term savings.

- The next step is to list your big expenses, such as your mortgage, loans, insurance, living expenses, and spending money.

- From today on, you need to have what we could call **EMERGENCY MONEY.** Emergency means just that, EMERGENCY. It is not there to redraw to prop up your overspending; it's for an emergency like your house being burnt to the ground. **Holidays and movie nights are not emergencies.**

  In the meantime, it keeps growing to secure your financial freedom. This needs to be in an interest-bearing savings account in a different bank or building society from where you have your daily spending money.

  Open your Emergency Account with $500 to $2,000, and then each week, a set amount is automatically transferred from your wages. You may choose to transfer 10% of your bring-home income or a set amount, which can be increased as your financial freedom grows.

  **Your emergency account says, 'I don't need to stress about money.' Good feeling.**

- The next step is to open two separate accounts. **Daily expenses** and **Savings.** Your DAILY EXPENSES account is where your income (100%) comes into, from which you have direct transfers to your Church Offering, your Emergency Money account, and your Savings account

(8%-10%, your decision). This should leave approximately 70%-80% in your Daily expenses account.

a. **Savings—This will help pay off outstanding debts, such as credit cards and other small and unnecessary debts, plus grow money for investment in property, a super fund,** or other assets.

b. **Daily Expenses – Divide 15% (your choice) into another two accounts as a subsidiary to your Daily Expenses account.** One is for **Fun** spending, holidays, outings, etc., and the other is for **Safety money** for unexpected things like Vet bills. This leaves 65%-70% for your regular bills (car, house, insurance, and living expenses).

As explained, you have the choice to adjust these amounts, but knowing the money is there each week and hasn't been wasted by overspending on something unnecessary (Fun money), will make you feel secure.

## Living Expenses

Some couples divide their living expenses on a spreadsheet into categories like food, car expenses, clothing, etc. This is purely a matter of choice but is not necessary. Remember that developing better daily routines and habits will soon become automatic, requiring less thought and conscious energy, resulting from not having to worry.

Just seeing the gradual long-term growth in your Emergency and Savings Accounts will give you the security of knowing that you are becoming a little bit wealthier every day. Scott Pape's book 'Barefoot Investor' is a book many couples have used to help them with their finances.

Remember, this is just a guide that you can work out together to suit your income. Always reduce living expenses where possible, but don't be stingy. Pay your way in life.

Set goals and enjoy the challenge and rewards. Remember that God is your provider. Philippians 4:19 tells us, *"And my God will meet all your needs according to the riches of his glory in Christ Jesus."* When we put God first in our lives and honour Him with our substance, He will provide.

Money and how we obtain it are gifts from God. *"Wealth and honour come from you; you are the ruler of all things"* (1 Chron.29:12). King David spoke these words because he honoured God and went from being a humble shepherd to becoming the King of Israel.

As your life moves forward, enjoy the benefits you have placed in your life through sound financial planning.

*"A faithful person will be richly blessed, but one eager to get rich will not go unpunished."* (Proverbs 28:20)

**Meditate:** God does not ask that you be successful, but he does expect that you be found faithful.

# REFLECTIONS

*"The greatest legacy one can pass on to one's children and grandchildren is not money or other material things accumulated in one's life, but rather a legacy of wisdom and faith."*
Billy Graham

## LIVING WITH PURPOSE

LIVING WITH PURPOSE will help you experience the joy of really having a meaningful relationship with Jesus Christ. Through these daily devotions, written from Dawn's experience of learning to listen and follow what God's Word teaches, you will find you experience the infilling of the Holy Spirit more deeply each day. Know God's blessing as you study His Word with the help of this special devotional book.

ISBN: 978-0-6457514-3-7
*Available Worldwide*

www.ingramcontent.com/pod-product-compliance
Lightning Source LLC
LaVergne TN
LVHW051126080426
835510LV00018B/2245